Public Expressions of Religion in America

Conrad Cherry, Series Editor

Published in cooperation with the Center
for the Study of Religion and American Culture
Indiana University–Purdue University at Indianapolis

Unsecular Media

Unsecular Media

Making News of Religion in America

Mark Silk

University of Illinois Press

Urbana and Chicago

Library of Congress Cataloging-in-Publication Data
Silk, Mark.

    Unsecular media : making news of religion in America / Mark Silk.

      p.   cm. — (Public expressions of religion in America)

    Includes index.

    ISBN 0-252-01904-0 (alk. paper)

    1. Journalism, Religious — United States — History — 20th century.

    2. Mass media in religion — United States — History — 20th century.

    3. Mass media — Religious aspects.   4. United States — Religion — 1960–
I. Title.   II. Series.

PN4874.S513A3   1995

070.4'492 — dc20   94–45939

                                                            CIP

For Ezra and Isaac,
half the men's club

"Tut, tut, child!" said the Duchess.

"Everything's got a moral,

if only you can find it."

LEWIS CARROLL

Contents

Preface

Anyone who knows something about anything is likely to be unhappy with the way it is covered in the news media. By the standards of those in the know, the media get it wrong, or slant it, or fail to put it in the proper context most or all of the time. When recipes for improvement are written, they inevitably call for more knowledge, more sophistication, and less bias on the part of reporters and editors. All this is as true of religion as of any other news beat—possibly truer.

But my aim in this book is not to sound the clarion for better religion coverage, although that is something devoutly to be wished. Nor have I set out to encourage better relations between those who cover religion and those who shepherd it, although both sides benefit when the encounters are civil rather than otherwise. In my view, good religion coverage should make religious leaders no happier than good political coverage makes politicians.

What I have tried to do is explore the ideas and attitudes that inform the news media's approach to religious subject matter, so that both journalists and their audiences may understand better why the daily story of religion reads the way it does. Such an understanding ought to help the journalists do their jobs better, while enabling the audiences to get more out of what the journalists do. It can also make clearer the place of religion in late-twentieth-century America. Although it might seem peculiar to look into news coverage for the meaning of religion in society at large, some things may be glimpsed darkly through that glass that have not yet been seen face to face. Or so it seems to me.

The book has a thesis, one that might seem peculiar as well. Contrary to the claims of other commentators and also popular opinion, I will be arguing that the American news media present religion from a religious rather than a secular point of view. This is not to ignore or minimize the tension between religion and journalism. The first chapter will make clear that such tension is intrinsic, resulting as much from the nature of the former as from the practices of the latter. Nevertheless, it is my contention that news coverage of religion in America can be properly understood only as the expression of values that derive from our religious traditions. As I will attempt to show, these values are embodied in a series of moral formulas, or topoi, that shape the way religion stories are conceived and written.

I have focused my attention primarily on daily newspapers and newsweeklies. Television news, as important as it is in supplying Americans with their regular diet of information about the outside world, operates under constraints of time that limit what it can do in specialty coverage areas like religion. The few systematic studies of religion news on television show little that differentiates it from print coverage, other than a certain proclivity for stories, like papal visits, that possess a strong visual component. From time to time, I leave the newsroom for a trip to the movies, where the images of religion usefully complement the journalistic perspective. Although I have not undertaken the kind of formal content analysis practiced by journalism scholars, I am thankful to have been able to profit from what others have done in this area. My approach is less scientific than humanistic and quasi-anthropological; I have tried to make what I could of my experience as a participant-observer on the staff of the *Atlanta Journal-Constitution*.

As a reporter, editorial writer, and columnist, I have written a fair amount about religion since I began working there in 1987. But I have never belonged to the sodality of full-time religion reporters and editors and feel some unease in criticizing the work of those laboring in that vineyard, often against deadline, with who knows what impositions from editors, headline writers, and copy desks. Fortunately, I am not about the business of tossing bouquets for good religion coverage and brickbats for bad. What concerns me are the cultural presuppositions that lie behind the coverage. In that regard (and lest I be told to put up or shut up), I have provided an appendix containing a handful of religion stories written by myself. These are intended not as models to be followed but as illustrations of how the categories I outline in fact functioned for one practitioner. Brief introductions describe the process in each case.

This is the work of a sometime intellectual historian who, by choice and luck, found himself earning a living in daily journalism—and who, for better or worse, has been unable to practice the craft without reflecting upon it. I am grateful to have been invited to indulge this weakness by Conrad Cherry of the Center for the Study of Religion and American Culture at Indiana University–Purdue University at Indianapolis. The experience of participating in the center's Lilly Endowment-sponsored project on Public Expressions of Religion has been all an author could wish, thanks to both the enlightenment of the public sessions and the warmth and acuity of our smaller working group. For three years this has been my invisible college.

At the *Journal-Constitution,* I would especially like to thank Doug Cumming, religion editor par excellence, for giving me leave, when I had the time, to play in the fields of the Lord; and Gayle White, as kind and generous a colleague as she is an exemplary religion reporter.

In this book as in all I write, I am indebted more than I can say to Leonard Silk—my father, teacher, moral inspiration, and friend. I wish he could have lived to see it into print. At home, and closest to my heart, is Tema Kaiser Silk, whose willingness to suffer a book alongside the daily grind of newspaper deadlines has been an act of love.

Part 1

Overviews

CHAPTER ONE

Whose
Prerogative?

Of all the institutions of American life, none demands such careful handling by the news media as religion. Government agencies, sports franchises, even corporations can be subjected to searching criticism and ridicule in the press and over the air. Churches are another matter. Not only are Americans a highly religious people, but, in contrast to the rest of the Western world, ours is also a country in which overt hostility to religion has not been legitimized by a tradition of anti-clerical politics. Religion stands outside the established order, at least officially, and woe to those who treat it with disrespect.

But if religion poses a special challenge to the norms of news coverage and commentary, it is not only because of the sensibilities of the American mass audience and the moral insulation afforded by the constitutional separation of church and state. When the news media set out to communicate religious subject matter, they run up against institutions jealously guarding what they take to be their own prerogative. For religions are themselves systems of communications—designed, in the first instance, to facilitate the exchange of information between the mundane world and the realm of the sacred.

Throughout history, human beings have used prayer and sacrifice to lay their concerns before their gods. Messages have come from the divine, or been presumed to come, by way of oracle, divination, miracle, prophetic utterance, mystical experience, and written text. Once received, those messages were passed along to others. In the West, more than elsewhere, it became religiously obligatory to communicate the messages of God to a wider public. Unlike the religions of antiquity from which they emerged, Judaism, Christianity, and Islam made religious knowledge inseparable from religious observance.[1] The God of Abraham had laws and concepts to communicate, and these in turn had to be relayed to the body of the faithful, and to those the faithful sought to win to their cause.

Nowhere did the dissemination of religious truth assume greater importance than in Christianity. Jesus himself is presented as the Word, the communication, of God.[2] The Christian scriptures are largely cast in terms of religious communication: Jesus as preacher, the disciples as spreaders of the faith, Paul as letter writer. The Gospels are literally God's Good News, and Christianity's Great Commission has been to disseminate that news as widely as possible. It is no wonder that from the advent of movable type to the epiphany of an electronic-information superhighway Christians have seized upon the latest technologies in order to evangelize the world.

But facilitating spiritual communication is only one side of the history of religion. Promiscuous traffic in religious messages can cause no end of trouble, particularly when individuals claim supernatural authority to tell others what to do and believe. The discernment of false prophets has been a persistent concern of Western religion since the days of the (true) prophets. From priestly offices and sacraments to creeds and tests of faith, religious leaders have evolved means of controlling the channels of spiritual communication and the meaning of what has been communicated. These instrumentalities are themselves generally held to be divinely ordained.

Inevitably, those who presume to speak without proper authorization of churches, communities of faith, doctrines, and practices will be viewed with suspicion. Indeed, ever since Paul's Ephesian converts burned their books on the "curious arts" (Acts 19:19), Christian churches have undertaken to regulate what was written about questions of faith and morals.[3] Through the Middle Ages, popes and church councils suppressed or condemned everything from apocryphal scriptures to works by heresiarchs to philosophical propositions advanced by licensed theologians. But the invention of the printing press upped the stakes immeasurably—as the Protestant Reformation soon made clear.

Armed with printed tracts, woodcuts, and, of course, Bibles, Protestant reformers waged communications war against all the ways and means of Roman Catholicism. In response, the papacy strengthened its regulatory efforts by issuing a formal *Index* of prohibited books to warn the faithful away from what was contrary to true belief. Catholics would later be assured that a book was not inimical by the sight of a bishop's *nihil obstat* (nothing stands in the way) and imprimatur (let it be printed).[4] Nor has the church's regulatory impulse disappeared in modern times. As the 1983 *Code of Canon Law* puts it:

> In order for the integrity of the truths of the faith and morals to be preserved, the pastors of the Church have the duty and the right to be vigilant lest harm be done to the faith or morals of the Christian faithful through writings or the use of the instruments of social communication; they likewise have the duty and the right to demand that writings to be published by the Christian faithful which touch upon faith or morals be submitted to their judgment; they also have the duty and right to denounce writings which harm correct faith or good morals.[5]

No institution likes its sins published; however, when it comes to religion, there is a tradition of not just blaming but demonizing the bearers of the bad news. In Roman Catholicism, their behavior comes under the rubric of Scandal, a sin that Aquinas defines as an unrighteous word or deed that occasions the ruin of another.[6] The idea is that sinful activity, if known to others, begets more sin. Part of the work of the devil, author of sin, is to make it known, to scandalize. Medieval preachers told of demoniacs who, possessed of the devil's knowledge, would go around disclosing the hidden sins of others. The scandal was avoided, however, if the sinner had confessed, for then the sin was wiped out of the devil's, and the demoniac's, mind.[7]

The worst kind of scandal was the kind that brought the church into disrepute, for that undermined the faith of the community of believers. To this day, not only does canon law specify ecclesiastical punishment for clerics who cause scandal by their misbehavior, but also, in certain cases, canonical penalties are to be suspended if these cannot be observed "without danger of serious scandal or infamy."[8] Better to let the punishment go by the board than to scandalize the faithful by publicizing clerical misdeeds.

Under these circumstances, it is scarcely surprising that the Catholic church's initial response to reports of child abuse by priests has been to hush them up. And when the news media have taken the stories and run with them, the church has not been happy. In 1992, Cardinal Bernard Law of Boston singled out the *Boston Globe* for its investigation of James R. Porter, who was accused of having molested dozens of children while serving as a priest in Massachusetts during the 1960s.

> The papers like to focus on the faults of a few. . . . We deplore that. The good and dedicated people who serve the church deserve better than what they have been getting day in and day out in the media.
>
> St. Paul spoke of the immeasurable power at work in those who believe. . . . We call down God's power on our business leaders, and political leaders and community leaders. By all means we call down God's power on the media, particularly the *Globe*. . . .
>
> It's time we take the bushel basket and the media off the light and let the light shine so all can see it.[9]

This perspective is not unique to Roman Catholicism. To take a Protestant example: In the 1970s, some independent charismatic churches developed a theory of "shepherding" that enhanced the authority of the pastor as governor of his flock.[10] Although the shepherding movement faded in the 1980s, its distinctive doctrine of "covering" survived and was embraced and elaborated by one of the largest independent charismatic churches in the Southeast, Chapel Hill Harvester (later known as the Cathedral of the Holy Spirit). At Chapel Hill, covering comprised a range of spiritual protections, including the obligation to refrain from disclosing the sins of the repentant. As one former member of the church put it, "If I know someone that is having trouble in a certain area, if he is trying to repent and change and I tell people what is going on, that is wrong."[11]

In 1992, the church's pastor, Bishop Earl Paulk, was publicly accused of having an affair with a member of the congregation, and stories began to circulate about an earlier (admitted) affair of his. As the scandal enveloped the huge church, Paulk distributed a letter to Sunday worshipers that shows the texture of the covering doctrine.

> I fight not to clear my name of my wrong doing [*sic*], for I am guilty of sin. But that sin has been forgiven and covered. It was interesting that they sought to drag out a sin from 33 years ago

this week to bring discredit to us. That sin was long ago admitted, confessed, forgiven and written about. In fact, it was the single issue that caused this ministry to be founded . . . a place of refuge and restoration for shepherds. Those who now dare drag it or any other sin out from under the Blood of Jesus Christ do so at the peril of their own souls.

The news media shared in this anathema. As Paulk wrote, "We did indeed want to keep this out of the press. It is obvious that the media always takes the adversary role against the church."[12]

Self-serving as the use of concepts like scandal and covering may sometimes be, it is nonetheless consistent with ancient doctrine regarding the spiritual significance of clerical misbehavior. Since the Donatist heresy of the fourth century, Christianity has taken the position that the sacraments do not depend for their efficacy on the moral purity of the minister. Those who disclose clerical immorality are in effect calling whole ministries into question and very possibly driving adherents away. (Paulk's church lost thousands of members as a result of his scandal.) The theological point is that the publication of church abuses may be considered morally culpable even if—perhaps, especially if—it is entirely accurate. When by their coverage the news media uncover sin in the bosom of a church, they tend to be seen by the church in question as doing the devil's work: the media not just as adversarial but as Adversary.

Needless to say, the news media take a very different view of their role. Journalists like to tell themselves that discovering wrongdoing and putting it on public view purifies rather than corrupts society, that journalistic truth sets people free, or at least enables them to free themselves. No matter that coverage of religion typically shies away from finding fault. The preponderance of celebratory and innocuous stories cannot overcome the strong suspicion that, as far as religion is concerned, the media are up to no good. For Americans cannot but sense the tension between the religion they profess and the news they imbibe. Leviticus 19:16 quotes the divine injunction "not to go up and down as a talebearer among thy people." What are the news media but talebearers?[13]

A final source of tension between religious institutions and the news media in the United States is the pluralistic religious environment within which the media must operate. Addressing a general audience that is religiously diverse, even a small local newspaper or a TV newscast in a tiny broadcast market will be obliged to obey rules that do not apply to a denominational newsletter or a TV evangelist reaching millions. Secular religion coverage cannot, at least overtly, favor one brand of religion over another. It must tread carefully in the presence of articles of faith and maintain a cautious distance from supernatural events. To the religious, this studied neutrality can look like indifference or worse. Yet it is worth considering the degree to which the constraints may reflect not a secular bias on the media's part but a common understanding of what is acceptable discourse in the public square.

Ever since it went on coast-to-coast radio in 1929, the Sunday broadcast service from the Mormon Tabernacle has been character-ized by preaching that might well take place in a mainline Protestant church and choral music familiar to the mass of American church-goers. Similarly, Fulton Sheen, the Catholic prelate who conducted the first and thus far only religious television show to appear on net-work television in prime time, purveyed generalized religious teaching rather than Roman Catholic doctrine—for which he received some criticism from Catholic conservatives.[14] To be sure, minority faiths—especially those historically subjected to as much hostility in Ameri-can society as Catholicism and Mormonism—might well be expected to downplay their distinctiveness in a bid for public acceptance or for reasons of self-protection. But it is clear from the experience of Faith and Values, the interfaith cable television network, that even majori-tarian religious bodies find it difficult to resist the common norms of operating in the public arena.

Faith and Values came into existence as Vision Interfaith Satellite Network (VISN) in the wake of the scandals involving televangelists Jim Bakker and Jimmy Swaggart in 1987. The impetus came from Tele-Communications, Inc., the nation's largest cable company, which felt, according to one executive, that the "quality of programming did not appeal to a broad range of our subscribers," and that "some of the devices for on-air fund-raising were inappropriate." Sensing a market for mainline religious fare among increasingly spiritually in-clined baby boomers, TCI met with religious leaders in New York and offered to pick up all expenses for service and distribution if member denominations provided the programming. To join, a denomination had to possess at least seventy-five thousand members and four hundred churches, and in short order Roman Catholic, Greek Orthodox, Unitarian, Jewish, Mormon, and an array of Protestant bodies signed on. Air time was apportioned according to the size of the denomination. Although the network made clear it did not want its members to water down their distinctive messages, it laid down certain rules: No on-air solicitation of funds and no maligning other faiths or seeking converts at their expense.

In October 1992, VISN entered into a channel-sharing arrangement with ACTS, the eight-year-old cable network of the Southern Baptist Convention. The merger with this manifestly multireligious enterprise created a small storm of criticism from Southern Baptists. In the past, America's largest Protestant denomination had stood apart from anything that smacked of ecumenism, and in recent years it had been dragged purposefully to the right by the internal victory of its conservative wing. For many Southern Baptists, "interfaith" meant something quite different from what it meant elsewhere. In the words of Darrell Robinson of the Baptists' Home Mission Board, "We have an interfaith witness program that deals with cults and false religion. The chief concern was that . . . Southern Baptist programs were interrelated with programs that we were opposing and exposing the heresies of."[15]

But unbeknown to the critics, ACTS itself had, from its inception, embraced a live-and-let-live interfaith policy similar to VISN's. As ACTS executive vice president Richard McCarthy said, "A pastor in his pulpit might say that Muslims and Jews don't have any hope of getting to heaven. But we would not want him to say it on ACTS." Why not? Evidently, there are truths that can be pronounced in the privacy of one's home or church that civility or public relations forbids even conservative Southern Baptists from saying on the public airwaves. Fundamentalistic as the Southern Baptist Convention had become, it was not about to attack Judaism or Islam (or Roman Catholicism) publicly as false religions, or to let such attacks go forth under its aegis. And so the criticism of the VISN/ACTS merger died away.[16]

Of course, not all American religious bodies choose to operate within the constraints. They pay a price, however, for refusing to conform. When an uncivil religion like the Nation of Islam repeatedly attacks Jews in classic anti-Semitic fashion, not only is it criticized by other religious bodies but the news media also join in, publishing the violations of civil speech and providing a forum for condemnation of the offender. Bound by rules of public religious discourse, the media help to enforce them as well. In this regard, a word needs to be said about the media's quasi-religious role as purveyor of values and supplier of contemporary rituals.

The usurpation of traditionally religious functions by the mass media in general and the news media in particular has been a common theme among media critics in the age of television. In *The Electronic Gospel*, written in 1969, William Kuhns argued that a milieu of entertainment had come to supplant the dominant religious-cultural milieu of earlier times. This new milieu, he said, provided its own priests in the form of a late-night TV host like Johnny Carson; its morality tales in cop shows like "Dragnet." Meanwhile, the church's sacred time had given way to prime time, within which the mythic structures of American culture were established. Kuhns was concerned to show the dangers television posed to bona fide religion: its inability to offer transcendence, its tendency to undermine belief in spiritual absolutes. The book ends with an exploration of what "the church" might do to counteract media influence and keep its own distinctive message alive.[17] A more recent version of this critique can be found in Gregor T. Goethals's *The Electronic Golden Calf*. A visual artist, Goethals sees the mass media as the only source of art that can provide the kind of spiritual encounter afforded by the religious art of the past. Like Kuhns, she looks for institutional religion to collaborate with artists to recapture some of the ground taken by the mass media.

Within this larger vision of media as religion, the critics have attributed special roles to the news media proper. "[N]ightly news programs map the cosmos with images that define for us the contours of reality," writes Goethals. "News commentators, like ancient priests, lead us through ceremonies that purport to represent and explain worldwide events."[18] Less grandly, Quentin Schultze notes how reporters eventually replaced early American pastors as New Englanders' "primary conduits" of news and views of the outside world: "Believing the pastors was a matter of faith and credibility, but so is trusting contemporary news reporters or advertisers."[19]

Not all such commentators treat media religion as a sign of the decline of the times. Indeed, the father of this genre of criticism, Marshall McLuhan, was prepared in 1963 to understand the latest electronic marvel in terms of the most transcendent religious experience of the Christian tradition: "Today computers hold out the promise of a means of instant translation of any code or language into any other code or language. The computer, in short, promises by technology a Pentecostal condition of universal understanding and unity." McLuhan even went so far as to postulate a communications medium capable of bypassing language altogether "in favor of a general cosmic consciousness."[20] But by and large, those who regard the media as performing religious offices are not happy about the fact; for them, the religion of media is a second-rate substitute for the real thing.

The religious offices that the media appear to perform demonstrate what the sociologist Robert K. Merton considered a latent (as opposed to a manifest) social function. That is, the media do not perform them intentionally to take the place of formal religion, but achieve that end as the unintended and unrecognized consequence of entertaining and informing the public.[21] Given the media's pervasiveness, such latent religious activity might well be seen as more indicative of the spiritual life of late-twentieth-century America than the traditional religious subject matter they manifestly display—especially if it were true that the media have supplanted religion as generators of social meaning. Whether that is so, however, is open to question.

Designating the media as the new ecclesia tends to overrate the power of religion in earlier societies while ceding too much to secular institutions in our own. The vast cultural disparities among societies that have adopted the same religion offer sufficient evidence of the existence of competing sources of social norms in the past. In Western society today, it is certainly the case that representatives of organized religion have ceased to control the main arteries of culture, but that does not prove that the mass media have been cut off from the influence of religion.

The argument here is to the contrary: To the extent they are concerned with religion itself, the news media, far from being cut off, are animated by particular religious values that are embedded in American culture at large. But before considering what these values are and how they shape the journalistic enterprise, it is necessary to trace the course of religion coverage in America in order to understand how it has changed and why contemporary observers misperceive what it is all about.

NOTES

1. Gedaliahu Guy Stroumsa, *"Paradosis:* Traditions ésotériques dans le christianisme des premiers siècles," in his *Savoir et Salut* (Paris: Cerf, 1992), 133.

2. It is of more than etymological significance that when one takes the Body and Blood, one is said to communicate. The Eucharist is the Word vouchsafed to all believers in common. Pope John Paul II noted the centrality of communication to Christianity when, in a 1987 address to a thousand national news and entertainment media leaders in Hollywood, he said, "For Christians, the communicating word is the expression of all reality as expressed by Saint John: 'In the beginning was the Word; the Word was in God's presence, and the Word was God' [John 1:1]." *Editor and Publisher,* September 26, 1987, 18.

3. For an account of such regulation within Judaism, see Moshe Carmilly Weinberger, *Censorship and Freedom of Expression in Jewish History* (New York: Sepher-Hermon Press, with Yeshiva University Press, 1977).

4. The desire to hold the press at bay was hardly limited to Roman Catholic authorities. In 1671, for example, a generation after John Milton's *Areopagitica* had effectively destroyed England's system for licensing and censoring the press, Governor William Berkeley of Virginia bluntly told the Lord Commissioners for Foreign Plantations: "Thank God there are no free schools nor printing, . . . learning has brought disobedience, and heresy, and sects into the world, and printing has divulged them, and libels against the best government. God keep us from both." Quoted in Jon Butler, *Awash in a Sea of Faith: Christianizing the American People* (Cambridge: Harvard University Press, 1990), 45.

5. *Code of Canon Law: Latin-English Edition* (Washington: Canon Law Society of America, 1983), Can. 823, §1.

6. *Summa Theologica* 2–2 q.43 a.1.

7. See Mark Silk, *"Scientia rerum:* The Place of Example in Later Medieval Thought," unpublished Ph.D. diss., Harvard University, 1982, ch. 8.

8. *Code of Canon Law,* Can. 1352, §2.

9. *Boston Globe,* May 24, 1992. Not all bishops have reacted this way, particularly as the extensiveness of the abuse sunk in. In 1993, Bishop Raymond A. Lucker of New Ulm, Minnesota, criticized fellow bishops for their handling of the issue in his diocesan newspaper. "[R]esponse from such leaders has looked like covering up, denial. Attempts at damage control have taken the form of manipulation of the press, resulted in lack of concern for families and for parish communities." Quoted in a Religious News Service dispatch, May 21, 1993.

10. The founders of the shepherding movement quickly took on the look

of spiritual authoritarians, drawing strong criticism from other charismatic and Pentecostal leaders. In the wake of various abuses, a number of the founders disavowed the entire approach. See Richard Quebedeaux, *The New Charismatics II* (New York: Harper and Row, 1983), 138–42; and Robert Digitale, "An Idea Whose Time Has Gone?" *Christianity Today,* March 19, 1990, 38–42.

11. *Atlanta Journal-Constitution,* December 5, 1992. The article is reprinted under number 4 in the Appendix.

12. Letter dated November 22, 1993. In author's possession.

13. Where the Constitution protects the news media so long as the information they publish is true, traditional Jewish law (for example) forbids the dissemination of true information (derogatory or otherwise) about others as an invasion of their privacy, except insofar as that information is needed to protect the interests of a third party or the larger community. See Alfred S. Cohen, "Privacy: A Jewish Perspective," *Journal of Halacha and Contemporary Society* 1 (1980): 53–87. In the Jewish mystical tradition, evil speech is condemned not only as corruptive of the speaker's soul but also as a blight upon the cosmos: "When the evil word ascends by certain paths . . . many [evil] spirits are aroused in the world, and a spirit descends from that side, for it has been aroused by that man with his evil word." Isaiah Tishby, ed., *The Wisdom of the Zohar: An Anthology of Texts* (New York: Oxford University Press, 1989), 1348.

14. One such was the Boston Jesuit Leonard Feeney excommunicated for disobedience after he persisted in teaching that there was no salvation outside the (Roman Catholic) church. Mark Silk, *Spiritual Politics: Religion and America since World War II* (New York: Simon and Schuster, 1988), 70–86.

15. *Atlanta Journal-Constitution,* April 3, 1993.

16. Ibid. This is not to suggest that addressing a general audience necessarily means stinting on one's religious distinctiveness. In fact, the perception of greater religious diversity can impel a more evangelical message. In a study of Billy Graham's long-running newspaper column, "My Answer," Charles H. Lippy found that by the late 1970s Graham's tacit assumption that those seeking counsel from him were Christians had "vanished, and the column had become a mechanism for evangelism." Unless the inquirer explicitly avowed Christian belief, Graham would end his answer with a call to conversion. Lippy, "Billy Graham's 'My Answer': Agenda for the Faithful," *Popular Culture* 5 (1982): 30.

17. William Kuhns, *The Electronic Gospel: Religion and Media* (New York: Herder and Herder, 1969).

18. Gregor T. Goethals, *The Electronic Golden Calf: Images, Religion, and the Making of Meaning* (Cambridge: Cowley Publications, 1990), 109.

19. Quentin Schultze, "Secular Television as Popular Religion," in *Religious*

Television: Controversies and Conclusions, ed. Robert Abelman and Stewart M. Hoover (Norwood: Ablex Publishing, 1990), 243.

20. Marshall McLuhan, *Understanding Media: The Extensions of Man,* 2d ed. (New York: New American Library, 1964), 84.

21. On the difference between latent and manifest functions, see Robert K. Merton, *Social Theory and Social Structure* (New York: Free Press, 1968), 114–36. For a discussion of how this distinction relates to religion, see Bryan Wilson, *Religion in Sociological Perspective* (New York: Oxford University Press, 1982), 27–52.

CHAPTER TWO

The Course
of Coverage

Journalism in America virtually began by giving offense to religion. The *New England Courant,* published by James Franklin with the assistance of various Boston literary rakes and his teenaged brother Benjamin, was the fourth newspaper in the Colonies but the first that was not of, by, and for public officeholders. Founded in 1721, the *Courant* was rowdy, satirical, and thoroughly iconoclastic — critical not only of the colonial government but also of the local clerical establishment, whose great figures were Increase Mather and his son Cotton. For its part, the establishment dubbed Franklin and company the Boston Hellfire Club.

His weekly broadsheet was scarcely off the ground when, taking the side of popular opinion, Franklin began a campaign against smallpox inoculation, which the Mathers were strongly supporting.[1] The assault provoked the eighty-two-year-old Increase to dash off a letter to the government's house organ, the *Gazette,* announcing how *"extreamly offended"* he was by the *Courant's* proprietor.

> In special, because in one of his *Vile Courants* he insinuates, that if *the ministers of God approve of a thing, it is a Sign it is of the Devil;* which is a horrid thing to be related! . . . I that have known what New-England was from the Beginning, cannot but be troubled to see the Degeneracy of this Place. I can well remember when the Civil Government would have taken an effectual Course to suppress such a *Cursed Libel!* which if it be

not done I am afraid that some *Awful Judgment* will come upon this Land, and the *Wrath of God will arise, and there will be no Remedy.*[2]

In fact, the *Courant* was investigated by a committee of the Massachusetts legislature, which concluded that the paper had both mocked religion and affronted the government. In due course, the Franklins were run off.

Perhaps reluctant to repeat their experience, American newspapermen generally steered clear of religion for more than a century. An exception was Nathaniel Willis, the publisher of a Jeffersonian newspaper in Ohio, and he was roundly criticized by his political associates in 1807 for including articles on religious subjects (mostly Methodist revivals). Yet despite the counsel of one adviser, who said he had never heard of religion in a newspaper, Willis was determined to practice Christian journalism, and in 1816 he helped inaugurate the *Boston Recorder* as a general-circulation Calvinist weekly.

The *Recorder* divided its pages equally between news of the world and news of religion, but as Marvin Olasky points out, "It would be a mistake to say . . . that part of the paper was secular and the rest religious, for all of it emphasized *God's* activity." Earthquakes were viewed as occasions for sinners to tremble and seek reconciliation with God. A recovery from illness was considered evidence of God's mercy. All kinds of stories, Willis wrote, gave "occasion to record many signal triumphs of divine grace over the obduracy of the human heart, and over the prejudices of the unenlightened mind."[3] Perhaps the closest equivalent in today's news environment can be found in Pat Robertson's "700 Club," where current events are reported and interpreted strictly according to the host's conservative-charismatic lights.[4]

Willis's *Recorder* was followed in short order by other religious newspapers, most of them linked to particular denominations, including the Methodists, Baptists, Presbyterians, and Unitarians.[5] The appearance of these journals was part of an explosion of Christian publishing during the 1810s and 1820s that amounted to the invention of the mass media in America. The New York-based American Tract Society and American Bible Society pioneered large-scale printing and papermaking techniques and devised distribution networks comprising dozens of local auxiliaries and traveling sales agents. In 1829, both societies declared a two-year goal of "general supply" — providing everyone in the country with the holy merchandise. Although that goal proved unattainable, nearly half a million inexpensive Bibles and New Testaments and more than ten million tracts were distributed nationwide, often on a door-to-door basis. By 1835, the missionary impulse of evangelical Protestantism had made "centralized, systematic mass publication . . . part of the American way of doing things."[6] Never had the American public been so inundated with a godly point of view.

But the tract and Bible societies did not have the field to themselves for long. By the 1820s, secular book dealers were pumping out cheap editions of James Fenimore Cooper and other popular authors. Then, in the mid-1830s, penny newspapers pioneered news for the masses with sensational and sometimes scurrilous accounts of life in the cities of Jacksonian America and effectively drove general-circulation religious newspapers like the *Recorder* out of business. As with the Franklins, the reinvention of American journalism by the penny press also began by directly affronting organized religion.

The creative genius at the birth of the mass-circulation daily was James Gordon Bennett, a journalist-provocateur whose Roman Catholic upbringing in Presbyterian Scotland left him with an abiding interest in religious matters and a blithe unconcern for accommodating his views to the local establishment. Bennett's hugely successful *New York Herald* changed the face of American journalism with splashy news of crime and sex, political muckraking, exposés of financial wheeler-dealing — and coverage of religion. His signal contribution was to treat religion as news, whether that meant stories on clerical immorality, new doctrine, conflict over the ownership of church property, or the entanglements of church and state.[7] And then there were the annual meetings that the nation's denominations (along with sister organizations dedicated to temperance, antislavery, and other worthy causes) were accustomed to hold in New York during May and June. These anniversaries, as they were called, had never been covered by the secular press, but were the exclusive province of religious weeklies reporting for their own denominational audiences. When the *Herald* began covering them as human dramas of moral commitment and ecclesiastical policymaking, clergymen as well as the religious press roundly denounced the secular intrusion into their spiritual domain.[8]

Besides straight-up news coverage, Bennett gave full scope to his own opinions on faith and morals, sparing no one who strayed from

his image of the spiritual straight and narrow. He skewered the Episco-
palians for their indulgence to wealth and power and attacked contemporary preachers as a class for inadequate learning, talent, and human
sensitivity. Although he regularly referred to himself as a Catholic and
was married in a Catholic church, he reserved his harshest words for
the religion of Rome. In a notorious essay, he made light of the doctrine of transubstantiation, then called for a "thorough reformation
and revolution in the American Catholic Church," declaring: "If we
must have a Pope, let us have a Pope of our own, — not such a de-
crepit, licentious, stupid Italian blockhead as the College of Cardinals
at Rome condescends to give the Christian world of Europe."[9]

In 1840, enraged by the *Herald*'s impiety, sensationalism, and muckraking, a holy alliance of Catholics and anti-Catholic nativists, busi-
nessmen, politicians, and rival publishers pronounced a Moral War to
drive Bennett out of business. The distinguished committee in charge
of the campaign threatened advertisers with a boycott if they didn't
pull their advertisements and asked hotel owners to close their doors
to anyone carrying a copy of the *Herald*. While Bennett won the Moral
War hands down, some historians have claimed that in its wake he
toned down his religion coverage. The only systematic study of the
subject demonstrates that he did nothing of the sort. It also shows
that his satirical assaults on religion were accompanied by neutral
and positive reporting.[10] For example, the year 1844 featured both an
ample supply of religious invective and the inauguration of regular
coverage of Sunday sermons. The latter at once enabled New York's
leading preachers to put their words before the masses and saddled
generations of young reporters with the job of taking them down.

The *Herald*'s religion coverage, if not its acerbic commentary,
quickly set the journalistic standard. Frederic Hudson, Bennett's long-
time managing editor, noted that after a few years those who had attacked the *Herald*'s invasion of the anniversaries "bitterly complained
if reporters were not sent to the meetings of the societies to which
they belonged."[11] Readers learned to expect religion stories to include
the kind of human interest that was Bennett's trademark. The persistent difficulty that the pious had with daily journalism was not how
religion itself was covered, but what all else was in the paper: the sensational crime news, the sex, the advertising for tobacco and saloons
and theaters. And so, efforts were made from time to time to create
daily newspapers that openly embraced Christian values and turned

down the offending advertising. *The North American,* started in Philadelphia in 1839, devoted its editorial page to edifying moral essays. In 1860, the New York *Sun,* first of the penny papers, was briefly reincarnated as a religious daily. The same year, the New York *World* came into being, complete with church notices on the front page, advertisements for sermon paper and Sunday school, and special rates for clergy. But despite circulation hopes based on the number of nominal Christians, the religious dailies failed time and time again.[12]

A significant cause of consternation among the more conservative clergy was the huge success of Sunday editions in the 1880s. In 1885, Dr. Howard Crosby directed a pastoral letter on the subject to his flock in the Fourth Avenue Presbyterian Church in New York City.

> We have seen with great sorrow the entrance of the Sunday newspaper into Christian families, and having witnessed the unhappy results of this admission, are desirous of warning you against the growing evil. The Sunday newspaper not only employs a large number of persons for its sale upon God's holy day, but it furnishes secular reading to divert the mind from the holy themes especially appropriate to the Sabbath. Our young people, who would not otherwise think of spending the day in such reading, are readily led to consider it a safe and proper thing, when they see the paper brought into the family, and even purchased from the stand by members of the church.
>
> There is no influence more insidiously seductive than this for the demoralization of our Christian households. Its air of respectability, the brief notice of some religious event in a corner of the sheet, the fact carefully proclaimed that the paper is not made up on Sunday, all furnish easy excuses to the conscience for harboring and encouraging that which unfits the mind for serious thought, which draws it away from God's Word, and which thus nullifies all the sacred influences of the Lord's Day. The mind thus led becomes filled with thoughts on business, politics, games, theatres, and crimes (which form the staple of newspaper literature). . . . The ungodly world rejoices in beholding the religion of Christ brought down to its own level, and Satan will use every effort, through the power of fashion, to accomplish this end. The Sunday newspaper is a powerful engine to achieve this result.

This screed was subsequently published by the *New York Times* under the headline "One of Satan's Engines" — in a Sunday edition.[13]

In fact, secular newspapers regularly set forth clerical pronouncements on questions of faith, morals, and public policy, and not only in the form of local sermons. After the Civil War, the leading national religious figures were Henry Ward Beecher, the voice of Victorian piety, and the fiery reformer Wendell Phillips. Phillips, Hudson points out, always made his communications "short, sententious, and severe, so that every paper can easily find room for them and copy them" — the nineteenth-century equivalent of sound bites. Estimating that both he and Beecher had millions of readers for their occasional prose, Hudson asked, "Are not these two men, therefore, the two great editors of the United States — the two journalists, *par excellence,* of America?"[14]

From the time they caught on to religion reporting, newspapers found some of their best copy in the revivals that regularly descended upon all parts of the country. Indeed, much of what we know of the rich and varied history of American revivalism comes from the extensive accounts published in the daily press. A revival was likely to be, in the smaller municipalities, the biggest show in town, and it was a show that offered the reporter the chance to review the performer, gauge his (or her) appeal, and mine rich veins of human emotion. It could also supply a measure of controversy, whether resulting from the hostility of some members of the settled clergy or from the revivalist's own attacks on local mores and institutions. For their part, revivalists relied on newspaper coverage to drum up public interest. Sometimes local papers would actually list the names of the people who hit the sawdust trail and shook the evangelist's hand.[15]

Bennett may have invented daily revival coverage in 1840 when he assigned a *Herald* reporter to write a series of lampoons on the controversial Baptist revivalist Joseph Knapp.[16] Almost two decades later, during the mini-awakening of 1857–58, he and his famous competitor Horace Greeley of the New York *Tribune* battled over who would provide the fullest accounts, with Greeley at one point devoting an entire issue to the revival. This elicited the approbation of the giant of nineteenth-century revivalism Charles Grandison Finney, who told an audience in Glasgow, "It ought to be said that the editor and proprietor of the New York *Tribune* has done much that has extended this work. He employed a special and an able Christian editor to collect and arrange the revival intelligence. . . . All honour to Mr Greely [*sic*] for the honourable course he pursued." [17]

Not that coverage necessarily signified enthusiasm. In a March 1858 editorial, the *Herald* took a dim view of the ability of the revival to reach the masses: "It is evident from this state of things, that the revivalists have not, so far, brought to grace those persons who need it most. They have captured a few clerks, a broken-down stock broker or two, a repentent pugilist, etc. . . . of the more genteel and idle classes — of those who are, or pretend to be, above the common working classes." [18] Such criticism, which drew upon the longstanding antirevivalist strain in American Protestantism, regularly found its way onto editorial pages. The Boston *Evening Transcript,* organ of Unitarian Brahmindom, sniffed at Dwight L. Moody for upbraiding as spiritually inert the very churches that were supporting him. The paper pronounced his Boston revival "wholly futile outside the range of the so-called evangelical churches." [19]

Yet the attacks were often compelled to give way to applause. When Moody, the greatest revivalist of his day, was in London with his famous vocalist Ira Sankey, the *New York Times* called them "vulgar" and "ignorant," but the paper did an about-face when confronted with Moody's Gotham revival of 1876: "The work accomplished in this city for private and public morals will live." [20] (Two decades later, the prospect of another Moody revival again elicited the *Times*'s skepticism: "[W]e are unable to believe that these meetings, if conducted on the lines made familiar by Mr. Moody, will be of any permanent advantage to the cause of religion.") [21] When the colorful Georgia Methodist Sam Jones returned to Nashville for a second citywide revival in 1885, the Nashville *Union* attacked his "coarseness, vulgarity, slang and positive misrepresentations," and professed amazement that he had been invited back to the city. But after Jones drew full houses three times a day for four weeks, the newspaper cried uncle, praising the "strange preacher" for attacking "the vices and immoralities of social life and the evil practices of church members like a frontiersman would fight a forest fire." It was not easy for mass-circulation newspapers to resist such demonstrations of mass appeal. [22]

Moody was not above promoting his efforts in the amusement pages of newspapers. "Some ministers think it undignified to advertise their services," he told his son. "It's a good deal more undignified to preach to empty pews." [23] But he was also prepared to sacrifice publicity for the sake of affecting more deeply a city's spiritual life. After 1878, he gave up preaching ten-to-sixteen-week crusades in central tabernacles and instead preached in several different churches over a six-month period. It was, however, precisely the shorter time span and the tabernacle that made his earlier revivals good news events; inevitably, newspaper interest flagged during his half-year marathons.

Jones, whose stock in trade was denunciation of personal immorality, wrote a regular column for the *Atlanta Journal* from 1892 until 1906, so it is hardly surprising that the *Journal* gave extensive coverage to the campaign he conducted in Atlanta in March 1896. It began with a front-page story on Monday, March 2, announcing that local ministers had split on whether to give their "indorsement" to Jones's crusade. Not that Jones needed the help. On Sunday, according to a story inside, the evangelist had opened the crusade in the downtown tabernacle that had been erected to accommodate Moody and outstripped Moody himself, drawing twelve thousand to what the newspaper predicted would likely be "the most memorable series of religious meetings ever held in Georgia." On March 4, the *Journal* ran a box at the head of its editorial column, announcing, "For the Next Thirty Days The Journal Everyday Will contain full and accurate reports of the Great Sam Jones Revival Meetings. See that you do not miss an issue." True to its word, the newspaper did not let an issue go by without reporting on Jones's efforts and announcing the schedule of events to come.

Like Moody before him, Jones was acutely aware of the benefits of newspaper publicity. He made a practice of reserving special seats on his tabernacle platforms for reporters, and he made good copy in Atlanta by holding services at Boys' High School, police headquarters, and the Western and Atlantic rail shops.[24] But that didn't prevent him from taking the Atlanta newspapers to task for running saloon and liquor advertisements and for uncovering personal scandals among the citizenry. While the *Atlanta Constitution* declined to report the criticism, the *Journal* took it in good humor, headlining its story on March 16, 1896, "Jones Roasted the Newspapers." He was, in fact, under no illusion about why he received the coverage he did. As the *Chicago Tribune* reported his words on March 12, 1886:

> The newspapers have aided me wonderfully in my work, yet I am satisfied they would not have given me such a reception if it

had not been for the vision of dollars they had before them. . . . Newspapers follow in the wake of public opinion rather than taking the lead, as is the general impression. While great newspapers are a great invention and absolutely indispensable, yet you never saw one in your life but that it was coldly and selfishly mercenary, ready at any and all times to rush along with the popular tide and follow willingly and anxiously every current or boom that arouses the country and increases their circulation. . . . They follow the boom and are following Jones.

When Jones finished his Atlanta crusade, the *Journal* summed up the month (under the headline "Sam's Task Is Done, Devil's on the Run" on April 2, 1896) with the claim that "no such moral event has ever happened in the city of Atlanta." How much its coverage was based on considerations of circulation is, perhaps, less clear than Jones believed. After the initial story on the ministerial endorsement dispute, the crusade never again made the *Journal*'s front page. No matter how large the moral import, a revival sermon was not front-page news.

Covering a potent revival often seems to have had an effect on the reporters themselves. The unnamed *Atlanta Journal* correspondent who followed Jones's 1896 crusade plainly shared the racial prejudices of his time and region. When Jones, who frequently designated services for particular audiences, preached to a full house of African Americans, the *Journal*'s March 16 story did not want for stock references to "an old fat auntie with sable face" and "the antebellum darkey with his crown of 'possum colored wool.'" Yet the spiritual power of the event drew the reporter beyond the racist conventions of the day. When the audience first filed into the tabernacle, they seemed, he wrote, "in doubt as to the real character of a 'white folks' meeting."

> This spirit of restlessness seemed to increase when books were handed to the singers on the stage and the jerky little songs suitable to the white folks were sung. When Mr. Tillman [Charles Tillman, Jones's singer and music director] came forward and asked all to join in a simple chorus, the restlessness began to die away . . . .
>
> The old song, "Jesus my all, to Heaven has Gone," with some variations, still further broke down the restlessness and nearly all joined in the familiar tune, making a subdued melody out

of which occasionally some deep bass would roll like the boom-
ing billow roars above the splashing of the wave on old ocean's
shore. . . .

Sam Jones waved his arms. The negroes understood and like
blackbirds rising from the newground they fluttered up from
their seats and the Rev. E. R. Carter, the well known colored
Baptist preacher, was asked to lead in prayer. It was a fervent,
heartfelt prayer that stirred the vast multitude like the wind sigh-
ing through the pines. . . .

Another negro song, "Let Me in the Lifeboat!" was sung at
which the Caucasian hearts beat faster and a glow suffused the
entire being of all who heard.[25]

Similarly, in his biography of Aimee Semple McPherson, Daniel Mark
Epstein shows how reporters' skepticism was overcome time and
again by the Pentecostal evangelist's personal magnetism and the
spiritual power of the healing services she conducted between 1919
and 1922. To cite but one account, written by Louise Weick of the *San
Francisco Chronicle:*

What followed beneath that tent in San Jose will probably sound
like the veriest hocus-pocus to many. But nevertheless it did
happen. It happened not in the misty, nebulous long ago, to
white-robed men and women in a time we cannot quite visualize
as ever having had reality, but to children and men and women
who had street addresses and telephone numbers, who came in
automobiles and not on camel-back by caravan, as it was said
they did long ago. The blind saw again; the deaf heard. Cripples
left their crutches and hung them on the rafter.[26]

Swayed by them or not, reporters drew upon revivals for the human
interest that was the stock in trade of Bennettian religion writing. Perhaps the greatest occasion for this kind of personal, impressionistic,
on-the-scene journalism was the Scopes trial of 1925, which was itself a
kind of revival. (In the spirit of the occasion, H. L. Mencken, the dark
scrivener of Scopes, ventured into the Tennessee uplands one evening
to provide his readers with an account of an actual camp meeting.)[27]
But the Scopes coverage was a kind of valedictory, for by the 1920s,
lively religion writing was on its way out, a victim of the rise of the

Saturday church (later, religion) page as a near-universal feature of American newspapers.

As early as the 1870s, some newspapers were publishing full church pages, complete with columns of religious announcements and syndicated features like the "International Sunday School Lesson," which offered a mainline Protestant perspective on the history and meaning of the Bible. (The name of this long-lived feature was changed to "The Bible Speaks" in the 1950s, when the National Council of Churches took it over.) Twentieth-century commercial considerations made the triumph of the church page all but inevitable. As churches multiplied in metropolitan areas, those that could afford it were impelled to promote themselves by advertising their Sunday worship services. For their part, the newspapers found it burdensome to list the many services gratis in smaller and smaller type and were delighted to jettison the lot in favor of boughten display advertisements.[28]

Thus religion news became a journalistic commodity like book and car news, with editorial content designed to accompany the advertisements on the adjacent page. Disinclined to bite the hand that fed it, the coverage of religion became increasingly bland and promotional; the Saturday page in effect solved the problem of journalistic impiety by creating a realm of sacred space where no one's faith or denominational identity would henceforth be put to the challenge. Scandals and other sorts of controversial matters were likely to appear, when they appeared at all, in other parts of the paper. According to a 1952 survey of religion editors, most of the copy used on their pages came directly from church press releases, a circumstance not unpleasing to those who sent the releases out. Of 1,500 Michigan clergy surveyed in 1960, 89 percent felt that the newspapers used most of what they supplied and 83 percent considered the coverage very or fairly complete. The church page was, in fact, their medium of choice for getting church news to the public.[29] From a journalistic standpoint, the Saturday page came to be seen as such a wasteland that to this day, where other specialty-beat reporters are enticed to new jobs by promises of dedicated science or education pages, religion reporters are promised the chance to write "for the rest of the paper." The church page is, in short, a ghetto from which the religion reporter hopes to be liberated.

But it was not simply the exigencies of commerce that led to the hegemony of the Saturday page and its promotional copy. In the increasingly staid, family-oriented, noncontroversial world of daily journalism, hard-edged religion coverage was increasingly unwelcome. Drawing invidious distinctions among religious bodies had always been problematic for American newspapers, but now, in the cities where the biggest papers were, it was no longer possible even to treat generic Protestantism as normative religion, at least explicitly. In a fractious world where ethnic political rivalries were colored with religious prejudice, mass circulation newspapers were anxious not to offend any denomination of readers with an ill-considered theological remark or an ecclesiastical exposé. All told, religion was trouble, and most editors wanted it to cut as inoffensive a figure as possible in their pages. As Lawrence C. Martin, the managing editor of the Denver *Post,* put it in 1940:

> Religion is a fruitful source of controversy; I mean by that the creeds, sectarian differences and denominational quibbles which are among the human perversions of true religion. In times past, newspapers got into so many scrapes over these religious squabbles that most editors drew in their horns and actually barred from their columns any but the most harmless and non-controversial items about churches or religious topics. Even today you will find most editors refusing to print letters from readers on religion, for fear of inciting to riot. Thus through the years there grew up, with good reason, a journalistic feeling that religion in the paper was dynamite.[30]

The handling of the dynamite predictably fell to pious newsfolk who could be depended upon to make sure that church announcements were accurately conveyed to the paper's readers. One such was Catherine Melniker of the *New York Journal-American,* who commented in 1951, "Our readers seem to appreciate the fact that the page is limited to city church news. We get many thank-you notes and no complaints."[31] Some did criticize the religion pages for ignoring religion news of the wider world.[32] Not that such news was unavailable. The Religious News Service, established in 1933 as part of the antiprejudice program of the National Conference of Christians and Jews, made use of hundreds of stringers at home and abroad, and in the early 1950s AP and UPI began to supply a steady trickle of the most important religion news, as well as annual features for holiday seasons.[33]

The conventional newsroom image of the religion editor is nicely captured in a scene from the "Lou Grant" television show, here recounted by the sometime religion editor of the *Charlotte Observer,* Terry Mattingly.

> As was often the case, Lou Grant was working on two problems at once. At first the problems seemed unrelated.
>
> The *Los Angeles Tribune* had lost its religion editor. City editor Grant had searched far and wide and, of course, no one was interested in the position. After all, what self-respecting journalist would want to be stuck with the religion beat?
>
> Problem number two was how to get rid of lazy, often-drunk, no-good reporter Mal Cavanaugh. All through this episode of "Lou Grant," the management of the *Trib* had been trying to find a way to get Cavanaugh to resign. Then, a spark of inspiration. The script is simple:
>
> LOU: Congratulations, Mal. You're the *Trib*'s new religion editor.
> *Lou sits back, beaming. The information seeps in a bit slowly on Cavanaugh, who blinks at Lou.*
> CAVANAUGH: Religion editor?
> LOU: That's right, Mal. And I can't think of a better man to interview the clergy . . . take ministers to lunch.
> CAVANAUGH: Are you kidding?
> LOU: Detail the theological frontier in this country and abroad.
> CAVANAUGH: That stinks! Before you stick me with a lousy job like that, I'd quit.
> LOU: Quit? You haven't even given it a chance. You can't quit.
> CAVANAUGH: The hell I can't. Just watch me.
> *Grant's newsroom associates beam as Cavanaugh storms out.*
>
> The television audience is left with the impression that Grant's problems are over. The religion editor spot is still empty, but who cares?[34]

In fact, a number of leading newspapers had, since the 1920s, employed serious and committed reporters to cover religion full time. Not infrequently, they were barred from conferences by church leaders mistrustful of their interest.[35] In 1949, a group of them formed the Religion Newswriters Association and, through the presentation of annual awards and discreet lobbying within the profession, began the process of enlarging and upgrading the beat.[36]

Their uphill struggle bore some fruit during the so-called Eisenhower revival of the 1950s, when religion at once rose in public prominence and became, in a sense, less controversial. Although the era was not without its interfaith skirmishes (mostly over Roman Catholic efforts to secure public education funds and an ambassador to the Vatican), the conviction became widespread that the entire Judeo-Christian community of faiths needed to make common cause in fighting the cold war. In 1960 Lillian Block, managing editor of the Religious News Service, summed up the state of religion coverage when she explained how "we attempt to demonstrate that religious news need not be 'explosive' if facts are presented with care." Then she added, "We continue to tell the story of how men of religion are seeking to combat with a spirit of hope and courage the defeatism and pessimism of those whose minds are beset by fears of atomic mass annihilation. . . . Day by day, RNS reports on the battle for the minds and souls of men in the struggle between the forces of democracy and Communism."[37]

Even advertisers put their shoulders to the wheel. In 1948, a campaign was launched to provide newspapers with ads promoting RIAL — Religion in American Life. The idea, which harked back to the early-nineteenth-century Bible- and tract-society goal of "general supply," was to reach every home in America with messages like "Find the Strength for Your Life . . . Worship Together This Week." In 1957, 888 newspapers ordered some eight thousand RIAL "ad mats" prepared by the J. Walter Thompson Co. The following year, a RIAL spokesman averred that newspaper support of the effort was a "key factor" in lifting church attendance 29 percent over the previous decade.[38]

Whether it was the ecumenical movement of the National Council of Churches or the theological punditry of Reinhold Niebuhr and Paul Tillich, religion did make good copy in the postwar world. The emblem of postwar religious promotion is the two-word telegram sent by the aged William Randolph Hearst to his editors at the *Los Angeles Examiner* when the young Billy Graham was leading a tent revival in 1949. "Puff Graham," it read. Likewise, in 1966 *Time* reacted with horrified piousness to the news that some American theologians thought God was dead.[39]

The high-water mark of postwar religion coverage was undoubt-

edly Vatican II, the Catholic church's great attempt at bringing itself
into the modern world. What could match the drama of Rome's children of light, led by the amazing Pope John XXIII, prevailing over
the children of the Dark Ages? Intrinsic to the story, at least from the
press's standpoint, was the breaking down of the Vatican's traditional
wall of silence. In the face of stiff bureaucratic resistance, correspon-
dents were able to learn what was going on behind closed conciliar
doors, and by accurate reporting, in the view of one clerical observer,
"did as much as any single group to alert the Catholic Church to the
necessity for dealing with modern mass media and their representatives in a modern way."[40] At the *New York Times,* executive editor
Abe Rosenthal never let subsequent religion writers forget what John
Cogley, who covered the latter phase of Vatican II, "did with the
beat." As Ari Goldman, one of the successors, recalled, "Sometimes I
thought that maybe what Rosenthal really wanted was another Vatican II rather than another Cogley."[41]

In a study of American newspaper coverage of religion from 1849
to 1960, Kenneth Nordin argues that, by presenting religion in increasingly standardized and generalized form, newspapers became a
major vehicle for the maintenance of an American religious consensus.[42] Although this may have been a premature judgment, reflecting
the united religious front that characterized the postwar period, the
degree to which the news media had managed to inoculate themselves
against religious criticism is nevertheless remarkable. In 1960, for example, a Catholic priest named Theodore Gerken was able to discern
no bias for or against any variety of faith in studying the religion coverage of the four metropolitan Chicago dailies then in the field. His
criticism, rather, was of the papers' reluctance to stake out editorial
positions on religious subjects. He noted that the occasional editorials the newspapers did publish on such subjects elicited little criticism
and argued in good Thomistic fashion that it was possible for editors
of the secular press to "discover generally accepted religious standards
and principles . . . from which the editorial writer can recognize the
limits within which he can make editorial comments." Such comments
would have more weight because of the newspaper's "non-partisan
position"—to Gerken, a good thing.[43]

Ecumenism was a good thing, Billy Graham was a good thing, Vatican II was a good thing. Religious support for the civil rights movement and religious opposition to the war in Vietnam would seem like

good things too. It was when religion no longer appeared to be always on the side of the angels that it once again became problematic for the news media to cover.

NOTES

1. See Michael G. Hall, *The Last American Puritan: The Life of Increase Mather, 1639–1723* (Middletown: Wesleyan University Press, 1988), 357–60.

2. Frederic Hudson, *Journalism in the United States from 1690 to 1872* (New York: Harper and Brothers, 1873), 67–68.

3. Marvin Olasky, "Democracy and the Secularization of the American Press," in *American Evangelicals and the Mass Media,* ed. Quentin J. Schultze (Grand Rapids: Academie Zondervan Books, 1990), 50.

4. For Robertson's interpretive approach, see Robert Abelman, "News on the '700 Club' after Pat Robertson's Political Fall," *Journalism Quarterly* 67 (Spring 1990): 157–62.

5. Abelman, "News on the '700 Club,'" 289–305. Hudson reports a total of 330 to 340 religious newspapers in 1872.

6. David Paul Nord, "The Evangelical Origins of Mass Media in America, 1815–1835," *Journalism Monographs* 88 (May 1984): 24.

7. James L. Crouthamel, *Bennett's New York* Herald *and the Rise of the Popular Press* (Syracuse: Syracuse University Press, 1989), 42.

8. Hudson, *Journalism in the United States,* 453.

9. Crouthamel, *Bennett's New York* Herald, 35.

10. Judith M. Buddenbaum, "'Judge . . . What Their Acts Will Justify': The Religion Journalism of James Gordon Bennett," *Journalism History* 14 (Summer-Autumn 1987): 54–67.

11. Hudson, *Journalism in the United States,* 453.

12. James Melvin Lee, *History of American Journalism* (Garden City: Garden City Publishing, 1917, 1923), 266–69.

13. It evidently did not occur to Dr. Crosby to condemn the Monday newspaper, which assuredly *was* made up on Sunday.

14. Hudson, *Journalism in the United States,* 301–2.

15. William G. McLoughlin, Jr., *Modern Revivalism: Charles Grandison Finney to Billy Graham* (New York: Ronald Press, 1959), 414.

16. Bernard A. Weisberger, *They Gathered at the River* (Boston: Little, Brown, 1958), 136.

17. Keith J. Hardman, *Charles Grandison Finney, 1792–1875* (Syracuse: Syracuse University Press, 1987), 431.

18. Marion L. Bell, *Crusade in the City: Revivalism in Nineteenth-Century Philadelphia* (Lewisburg: Bucknell University Press, 1977), 192.

19. McLoughlin, *Modern Revivalism,* 241, 266.

20. Ibid., 241, 266.

21. James F. Findlay, Jr., *Dwight L. Moody: American Evangelist, 1837–1899* (Chicago: University of Chicago Press, 1969), 403.

22. McLoughlin, *Modern Revivalism,* 287.

23. William R. Moody, *The Life of D. L. Moody* (New York: Fleming H. Revell, 1900), 426.

24. McLoughlin, *Modern Revivalism,* 303.

25. The *Atlanta Constitution* also featured an extensive account in a similar vein in its March 15 issue.

26. Daniel Mark Epstein, *Sister Aimee: The Life of Aimee Semple McPherson* (New York: Harcourt Brace Jovanovich, 1993), 229–30.

27. Reprinted in Alistair Cook, ed., *The Vintage Mencken* (New York: Vintage Books, 1956), 153–61.

28. This account of the evolution of the religion page relies on Kenneth Dayton Nordin, "Consensus Religion: National Newspaper Coverage of Religious Life in America, 1849–1960," unpublished Ph.D. diss., University of Michigan, 1975, ch. 4.

29. *Editor and Publisher,* April 16, 1960, 39. The rise of the Saturday page was accompanied by a decline in regular weekly sermon coverage, because no self-respecting daily would publish reports of Sunday sermons six days later. The disappearance of traditional Monday sermon space was doubtless helped along by radio broadcasting, which prominent and aggressive pastors quickly seized upon to lay their words directly before the general public. In the 1920s, the Sunday morning radio dial was filled with preaching. Why print excepts of what people could hear for themselves? The *New York Times,* always reluctant to give up old features, maintained its sermon coverage into the 1960s, but it was one of the last.

30. Quoted in Arthur Robb, "Shop Talk at Thirty," *Editor and Publisher,* April 27, 1940, 106. In 1958, the AP's George Cornell told *Editor and Publisher,* "Religious discussion is barred from schools[,] and newspapers for many years regarded religion as a private affair and stuck to superficial coverage of routine church announcements of sermon topics. Newspapers were afraid they might offend." December 27, 1958, 12.

31. *Editor and Publisher,* November 24, 1951, 52.

32. "Time and time again, religious leaders have criticized newspaper religious news sections for their emphasis on local news to the neglect of national and international developments in religion." Comments of Willmar Thorkelson, religion editor of the *Minneapolis Star,* in *Editor and Publisher,* July 23, 1960, 50.

33. Every Christmas and Easter, AP religion writer George Cornell was "confronted with the assignment of how to retell some aspect of the Chris-

tian story after 2,000 years and many versions and repetition." *Editor and Publisher*, December 27, 1958, 12.

34. Terry Mattingly, "The Religion Beat," *The Quill* (January 1983): 12.

35. John Evans, who covered religion for the *Chicago Tribune* from 1929 through 1956, encountered Protestant hostility because of his paper's vehement stand against Prohibition. *Editor and Publisher*, March 17, 1956, 40.

36. See George Cornell, "The Evolution of the Religion Beat," in *Reporting Religion: Facts and Faith*, ed. Benjamin J. Hubbard (Sonoma: Polebridge Press, 1990), 20–35.

37. *Editor and Publisher*, July 23, 1960, 50.

38. *Editor and Publisher*, November 8, 1958, 30.

39. See Frederick D. Buchstein, "The Role of the News Media in the 'Death of God' Controversy," *Journalism Quarterly* 49 (Spring 1972): 82.

40. James W. Whalen, "The Press Opens Up Vatican II," *Journalism Quarterly* 44 (Spring 1967): 53.

41. Ari Goldman, *The Search for God at Harvard* (New York: Random House, 1991), 198.

42. Nordin, "Consensus Religion," ch. 6.

43. Theodore Gerken, "Religious News Policies and Procedures of the Chicago Metropolitan Newspapers," unpublished M.A. thesis, Marquette University, 1960, 183–85.

CHAPTER THREE

The Phantom
of Secularism

When Sam Jones roasted the Atlanta newspapers during his 1896 revival, he didn't shy away from addressing the men in charge.

> Presbyterian elders, Baptist deacons and Methodist stewards
> own the two leading dailies of the city, and if the devil had
> planked down the cash and bought out the whole thing, with
> the goods delivered, they could not do his service more effectu-
> ally in many ways.
> Their advertisement of saloons and liquors and the publica-
> tion of scandals, which has in more than one case driven some
> victim to suicide and to hell, appear in these papers; and there
> are some little reporters like scavengers of hell destroying char-
> acter and breaking the hearts of the good mother and father at
> home. And they stick this in. This may be legitimate newspaper
> work in this 19th century, but I prefer that the devil would put
> his own crowd at it, rather than the elders and deacons and stew-
> ards of the church, and make them the owners of the thing and
> have them divide the profit of the thing.[1]

Jones understood full well that newspapers were in business to make
a buck; that, folks being susceptible to alcohol and titillation, it was
good business to trade in sin. Yet although publishers might be doing
the devil's work, they were nonetheless Christians who could be made
to feel guilty for the way they earned their bread.

By contrast, a present-day evangelical activist like the antiabor-

tion crusader Tim LeHaye sees purveyors of news as the devil's own
crowd, irreligious adversaries who corrupt the nation not for the love
of money but out of immoral conviction.

> It's no secret to any of us how the liberal media manages the
> news and helps to set the national agenda on public debate. They
> report the news in such a way as to promote the political goals of
> the left. The censorship of Christian principles and ideas covers
> many more issues than abortion and the homosexual lifestyle.
> The media slants what is reported in the areas of national de-
> fense, the budget, school prayer, and Soviet expansion in Central
> America, among others. The truth in all these areas is being hid-
> den.[2]

Are the news media hostile to religion? Nowadays, many seem to
think so. In order to see how Sam Jones's complaint metamorphosed
into Tim LeHaye's, we must trail the phantom of secularism through
changing images of the media and American society in the twentieth
century.

After World War I, the proposition that America was becoming an
increasingly secular society gained wide acceptance. In *Middletown,*
their influential 1929 study of a small American city, Robert and Helen
Lynd registered a significant decline between 1890 and 1924 both in
church and Sunday school attendance and in the overall pervasiveness of religious life. Evidence for this picture of secularization also
came from calculations of the amount of attention paid to religion by
the local press. Comparing a week in 1890 with one in 1923, the Lynds
found that the average amount of religious subject matter in Middletown's two newspapers declined from 5.6 percent to 2.3 percent.[3]

For the nation as a whole, the sociologist Hornell Hart found that
of the articles catalogued in the *Reader's Guide to Periodical Literature,* the proportion dealing with religious subjects dropped 50 percent (from 2.14 to 1.07) between 1905 and 1930. Not only that, but
in comparing positive and negative views expressed in a sample of
these articles, Hart also calculated a decline in approval of traditional
Christian beliefs and practices from 78 percent in 1905 to 33 percent
in 1930. The rate of approval of church and ministers similarly went
down, from 61 percent in 1905 to 20 percent in 1930. On the strength
of these findings, Hart predicted a "probable further decline of inter-

est in traditional Christianity" and found exactly that in a follow-up study showing that, between 1931 and 1941, the proportion of magazine articles on religion declined even faster than before. Hart correlated the small decreases in the percentage of the population belonging to churches and going to Sunday school with polls in which respondents indicated they thought religion had become less important. All in all, he concluded, organized Christianity was on the wane in the United States.[4]

Despite the post-World War II resurgence of interest in religion, the secularization hypothesis managed to hold its own through the 1970s, supported by some newspaper content analysis. For example, in a decade-by-decade study of religious content in the *New York Times* between 1865 and 1975, Robert Pettit detected a sharp drop-off in the prominence of religion around the turn of the century and an ongoing decline thereafter. Although the percentage of religious news space more than doubled from 1945 to 1955, Pettit denied that this was statistically significant, and in any event he was able to show that by 1975 religious news space had reached its lowest ebb in *Times* history.[5]

But the image of implacable secularization in the news media did not go unchallenged, especially as the century drew to an end. Systematically sampling dozens of daily and weekly newspapers in the years 1849, 1874, 1904, 1931, and 1960, Kenneth Nordin found a decline in religion news on the front page but little variance in the total amount of news space devoted to religious subject matter.[6] In 1958, a survey of 134 church editors by the Religious Newswriters Association disclosed that 98 percent of newspapers put religion news on the front page, and that nearly half had instituted church pages since World War II.[7] A study of religious content in popular magazines from the late 1930s to the late 1970s concluded that "a small but continuing stream of religious material seems to reach public attention through this form of mass media."[8] This last study, indeed, indicated that references to religion increased fourfold between the early and the late 1970s in the two American publications studied (*Reader's Digest* and *Saturday Review*). A 1982 survey of religion editors and reporters at thirty newspapers indicated that during the previous decade the number of papers devoting more than one hundred column inches to religion had more than doubled, from 27 percent to 59 percent.[9] By 1989, Stewart Hoover, Barbara M. Hanley, and Martin Radelfinger in

a Religious News Service–Lilly Endowment study of religion reporting and readership could speak without fear of contradiction of the
"new prominence of religion in the news."[10]

The religion news that came to the fore was different from what had
gone before—less institutional and altogether more troubling. Looking back to his early years in journalism, Ari Goldman noted the shift:
"By the time I became a *Times* reporter, the religion beat had less to
do with big institutions like the Vatican and more to do with religion
as a countercultural movement. From reading the newspapers of the
late 1970s, it would seem that the greatest threats to young middle-
class Americans were Eastern religious cults."[11] There was also the
so-called born again movement, symbolized by Jimmy Carter, which
appeared cultlike to those unfamiliar with the language and practices
of evangelical Protestantism. It evolved journalistically into the Christian Right, which by the early 1980s was receiving so much ink and air
time that some wondered whether Jerry Falwell and company weren't
simply a creation of the secular news media.[12] The televangelist scandals of 1987, the pedophile scandals in the Catholic church, and the
1988 presidential campaigns of the two ministers, Jesse Jackson and
Pat Robertson, kept religion on the front burner in the late eighties.
Meanwhile, from the seizure of the American embassy in Tehran during the Shiite revolution in Iran, the revival of Islam as a spiritual and
political force became a major, ongoing story. Nor, after the collapse
of communism, could the revival of religion in the former Eastern
bloc be ignored, whether as a source of spiritual sustenance or as a
force for ethno-religious warfare.

This increased salience of religion in the United States and abroad
tended to undermine the secularization hypothesis in favor of the
views of sociologists like Andrew Greeley, who argued as far back as
1972 that statistical data "simply *do not* indicate a declining religious-
ness in the United States."[13] Yet the hypothesis' loss of favor did not
lead to a new appreciation of the media's role in conveying news of
religion to the public. On the contrary, the news media began to draw
increased criticism for being agents of the very secularizing forces they
were now reporting to be in retreat.

From the early studies of media secularization, the assumption of
scholars had been that trends in religious news space expressed trends
in society at large. In Pettit's cautious characterization, "Since the concerns and attitudes of press and public are probably correlated, it is a

reasonable hypothesis that newspaper content is a valid indicator of at least some aspects of social change."[14] But this probable correlation was challenged in 1981 by Robert Lichter and Stanley Rothman in the collective portrait they drew of an American "media elite," based on interviews with 240 journalists and broadcasters at the *New York Times, Washington Post, Wall Street Journal,* the three news weeklies, the three major television networks, plus PBS and other major public broadcasting stations. A "predominant characteristic" of this elite, Lichter and Rothman said, was its "secular outlook." Half had no religious affiliation. Only one in five was Protestant; one in eight, Catholic. Eighty-six percent seldom or never attended religious services. These and other findings finally put some empirical flesh on bones that conservative critics had been picking with the "liberal media" for some time. To be sure, Lichter and Rothman did not conclude from their findings that the media elite presented a biased picture of the world. ("The crucial task that remains is to discover what relationship, if any, exists between how these individuals view the world and how they present that world to the public.")[15] But where they remained agnostic, others professed belief.

Jerry Falwell seized upon the study as documenting "what most of us already suspected" and opined, "Far from reflecting what the public thinks, the press reflects what it thinks — what it believes is the right course for America to follow. No wonder those who are trying to call America back to her moral and spiritual traditions and heritage are so often ravaged by columnists and excoriated by network reporters."[16] Falwell did not lack for the company of more intellectual polemicists. In *The Naked Public Square* (1984), Richard John Neuhaus entertained not the slightest doubt that the reality conveyed by the media and the reality experienced by the populace at large were two profoundly different things: "The point is that the widespread exclusion of religiously grounded values and beliefs is at the heart of the outrage and alienation (to use a much overworked term) of millions of Americans. They do not recognize *their* experience of America in the picture of America purveyed by cultural and communications elites. At the heart of this nonrecognition — which results in everything from puzzlement to crusading fever — is the absence of religion."[17] In his book on the 1988 presidential election, Garry Wills chastised editors and reporters for shying away from "political coverage of religion," the result, he claimed, of religious ignorance and the fear that this would "somehow breach the wall of separation between church and state."[18] In his near-hysterical assault on the movie industry, *Hollywood vs. America,* Michael Medved contended that the "negative attitude toward Judeo-Christian believers is so pervasive and so passionately held in Hollywood that some producers will use every opportunity to express their contempt."[19] And in *The Culture of Disbelief,* a book warmly embraced by President Clinton, Stephen L. Carter charged the news media with highlighting religiosity in politicians they dislike (those on the right) but ignoring it in those of whom they approve.[20]

In a curious way, the effect of this criticism was to keep the secularization hypothesis alive; but now, instead of applying to American society as a whole, it attached to those in the business of representing it. By the end of the Vietnam War, emergent neoconservatives had begun denouncing journalists, academics, and other "meaning-generating" professionals as members of a New Class that was middle class in income but hostile to middle-class values.[21] By the 1990s, it became common to speak of American culture as a war zone divided between orthodox believers of all faiths and New Class humanistic liberals. Instead of serving in the vanguard of a secularizing society (as Hornell Hart viewed magazine readers before World War II), the members of the New Class came to be seen as profoundly alienated from the values of ordinary, church-going Americans. It was a characterization that accorded nicely with the longstanding tradition of anti-elitism in America, which since the Great Awakening has often charged elites with irreligion.

It was also demonstrably a point of view that the religious public at large embraced. Of one hundred Catholic priests in Pennsylvania surveyed in 1986, only 19 percent considered news stories to be "fair, honest or objective."[22] In Hoover, Hanley, and Radelfinger's RNS–Lilly survey, most people interviewed in four Philadelphia congregations felt the press had "some sort of a 'bias' against religion," although they disagreed over whether it was an active bias against particular faiths or simply the product of ignorance and indifference.[23] Similarly, in John Dart and Jimmy Allen's 1993 Freedom Foundation report on religion and the news media, a large majority of the 529 clergy surveyed agreed either "strongly" or "somewhat" with the following statement: "Most religion coverage today is biased against ministers and organized religion." Specifically, mainline Protestant clergy agreed by a margin of 58 to 19 percent (with the remainder noncommittal), while Catholic priests and "conservative Christians" agreed by 70 percent and 91 percent, respectively.[24] This would seem to reflect a significant shift from the early 1960s, when, for example, comments about newspapers and magazines in religious journals were, according to one study, "largely neutral."[25]

But is the late-twentieth-century image of the media as implacably secular true? In 1970, *Christianity Today* surveyed religion editors across the nation and discovered a high degree of religious commitment on their part. Of 180 respondents, 146 said that they belonged to some religious body; 83 percent said that they believed "in the reality of God."[26] A quarter-century later, the survey conducted for the Dart-Allen study showed, if anything, stronger religious commitment. Of 99 religion writers, only 4 percent indicated no religious affiliation; and of 266 editors, only 9 percent. Seventy-five percent of religion writers said religion was "very important" to them, and 72 percent of editors said it was either "very important" or "somewhat important." Not surprisingly, the journalists, by a three-to-one margin, denied being personally biased against religion.

Comprehensive surveys of journalists nationwide conducted in 1971 and 1982–83 tended to bear this out, showing a rate of religious affiliation nearly identical to the population at large. The only notable divergences were a moderately higher proportion of Jews in the news media (about 6 percent compared to 2 percent of the population as a whole) and a smaller proportion who professed either no religious affiliation or something other than Protestant, Catholic, or Jew (about 7 percent compared to 11 percent). While admitting that Lichter and Rothman's "elite" might be more secular than the rest of American society, David Weaver and G. Cleveland Wilhoit questioned how much influence they might have over other news organizations, as well as how much such a demographic fact affects news values.[27] Yet if members of the media were not disproportionately secular, what of the coverage itself? Where two-thirds of the clergy in the Dart-Allen study felt that most news of religion presented an "unfairly negative picture" of clergy, churches, and faith, two-thirds of the journalists disagreed. These results, Dart and Allen said, represented a "bone-chilling difference of opinion over whether news coverage is slanted against religion."[28]

Setting aside for the moment the conundrum of bias, what about the question of quality? One study, based on a 1986 survey of religion editors at newspapers with circulations of a hundred thousand or more, concluded that religion coverage had increased in both quality and quantity. Conclusions based on the responses from journalists may naturally be open to question (although given the eternal newsroom laments over lack of space and appreciation, any declarations of improvement could as likely be understatements as overstatements). In any event, in a study of religion coverage that did not depend on journalists' self-assessment, Judith Buddenbaum judged that, as of 1981, religion news stories in the *New York Times,* Minneapolis *Star,* and Richmond *Times-Dispatch* had become "longer, broader in scope and more issue-oriented than they once were."[29]

But what of television, which many Americans depend upon as their main source of news? A study by the conservative Media Research Center pictured national television newscasts in 1993 to be a religion wasteland. In evening news shows on CNN, PBS, and the three networks, religion was found to be the focus of just 1 percent of all news stories, and then, according to the authors, was often scorned.[30] However, other studies show a less bleak image. Where the Media Research Center excluded major news events "involving a religious angle," including the Branch Davidian siege in Waco and the World Trade Center bombing, which religion newswriters ranked first and sixth among the top religion stories of the year, Buddenbaum drew her net much more widely in examining sample network news broadcasts from 1976, 1981, and 1986. By her count, ABC, CBS, and NBC news mentioned religion in 6 to 11 percent of their stories, consuming 7 to 15 percent of available air time. Religion was not the subject of most of these, but instead came up, as relevant, in the context of general news coverage. While discovering cases of biased reporting, Buddenbaum concluded that treatment of religion was generally fair.[31]

Laying the views and overviews of religion coverage one on top of the other, we are left with an indistinct portrait. Journalists appear about as religious as the population at large, although perhaps not those journalists occupying the most prestigious positions. The amount of attention given to religion in the news media may or may not have changed since the mid-nineteenth century, but seems to be on the rise toward the end of the twentieth. Exactly what the amount of religious news space signifies is far from clear, but it would appear to matter less than how the space is actually used.

Formal content analysis tends to sort stories into thematic categories of subject matter (beliefs, trends, and events) and news value (conflict, consensus, human interest, and novelty). The discovery that conflict stories play a large part in religion coverage (as in coverage of all news) has sometimes been taken to indicate bias against religion, as though the existence of conflict is antithetical to the true story of religion. (Adding up the number of conflict versus consensus stories in biblical narratives might suggest otherwise.) Overall, these categories offer limited insight, in part because the coding process on which they rely is designed to minimize the need for researchers to exercise judgment in analyzing texts. They can do little, for example, to differentiate important stories that may express a major commitment on the part of a news outlet from run-of-the-mill coverage that editors (and the public) hardly notice. In short, as useful as its findings are, content analysis seems capable of going only so far toward making sense of how the news media reckon with religion.

Perhaps the most strenuous effort to go farther is Lichter, Amundson, and Lichter's 1991 survey of coverage of the Catholic church by the *New York Times, Washington Post, Time* magazine, and CBS during three five-year periods in the mid-1960s, 1970s, and 1980s. Commissioned by the Knights of Columbus and the Catholic League for Religious and Civil Rights, the study attempts to answer empirically the question that Lichter and Rothman posed: Does the elite's secularist personal background affect its coverage of religion? Stories were grouped into four subject areas found to have dominated the coverage: sexual morality, power relations within the church, relations between the church and state authority, and relations with other churches. In all but the last area, the study concluded, the church was on the losing side of a policy debate. In addition, the authors assessed the media's use of descriptive language and found that the church was "overwhelmingly portrayed as an oppressive or authoritarian institution." The basic story line, they concluded, "increasingly . . . revolves around a beleaguered authority struggling to enforce its traditions and decrees on a reluctant constituency."[32]

As striking as the study's conclusions are, they were immediately called into question by the lay Catholic magazine *Commonweal* in a lengthy lead editorial entitled "Thin-skinned." The magazine pointed out that of the 1,876 stories sampled by the study, only 115 used "emotive" words like *authoritarian, rigid,* or *emancipating* to characterize the church as either oppressive or liberating. That 98 of the 1,876 used "oppressive" terms hardly justified characterizing the portrayal of the church as overwhelmingly oppressive. The magazine also criticized the study's method of comparing the number of "positive" and "negative" quoted statements in a story (not including official church pronouncements) to determine whether the church came out ahead or behind in the debate. The study had explained this approach by displaying its analysis of a *New York Times* story on the Vatican's silencing of the controversial West Coast theologian Matthew Fox. That story included a number of harsh characterizations of the church by Fox, thus putting the church on the losing side, according to the study's analysis. But, as *Commonweal* noted, the story's lead paragraph was written in such a way as to call into question all that Fox had to say. ("An obscure Roman Catholic priest, popular on the New Age lecture circuit, but about to be silenced by the Vatican, today cast himself in the mold of Galileo, St. Thomas Aquinas, and other Catholics who have been disciplined over the centuries.") Fox's supporters could well have concluded that the *Times* was biased against him, not the church. Finally, *Commonweal* disputed the study's identification of "the church" solely with certain official positions or attitudes, as if Vatican II had not construed it as the whole people of God. A close look at the actual findings, the magazine concluded, shows an "overall picture . . . painted in shades of gray rather than in the black-and-white of winning and losing sides."[33]

Commonweal may have protested a shade too much, but its criticism of Lichter, Amundson, and Lichter can hardly be considered secular. It is based, rather, on a different understanding of the church, one encouraged by Vatican II, if fallen somewhat into disfavor during the papacy of John Paul II. Clearly, its sense of the basic story line of American Catholicism was closer to the media's than to public pronouncements by the church hierarchy. Who is to say whether that story line is biased or true, secular or spiritual?

When John Paul II journeyed to the United States for the first time in 1980, it was to a virtually unanimous chorus of adulation from the news media. After the celebratory smoke had cleared, Garry Wills—a lay Catholic of considerable theological background—took to the pages of the *Columbia Journalism Review* to excoriate reporters and commentators for abandoning all serious journalistic coverage and reflection and giving themselves over to "papolatry." Willing self-censorship had blocked out, he said, such important matters of controversy within the church as the ordination of women and the fact that most American Catholics did not subscribe to the church's teaching on birth control and abortion. The press's reverential attitude was "implicitly condescending to religion, reducing it to fairy-tale status."[34]

Several papal visits later, the news media finally caught on—or did they? During John Paul II's 1993 journey to address a Catholic youth rally in Denver, church dissidents were regularly quoted. Troublesome matters like the priest shortage and the child-abuse scandals were regularly brought up. With reverential self-censorship out the window, inevitably came the criticism. Three conservative Catholic organizations accused news organizations of focusing unfairly on the dissent of "non-practicing" Catholics (a charge Gallup disputed).[35] The Media Research Center asserted that network television stories "had a distinctly negative tone," with sound bites that challenged the church's "theological rigidity" outnumbering defenses fifty-seven to twenty-seven. And in the *New York Times,* Peter Steinfels (sometime editor of *Commonweal*) lamented the focus on issues that were, at least to him, overly familiar. The pope, he claimed, had things to say about moral absolutes in a relativistic culture that were newer and more interesting than the old stories about a troubled church.[36]

Were the news media that followed the pope in 1993 engaged in the kind of noncondescending religion coverage that Wills was looking for? Or had they, in hewing to the past decade's main storyline, missed the real story? In the final article of a 1994 *New York Times* series on the Catholic church, Steinfels, the most knowledgeable and sympathetic of observers, suggested on June 1 that the main storyline was right ("Future of Catholicism Worries Catholic Leaders"). Ultimately, this is a question for informed judgment, not content analysis. However it is answered, the concept of "secular bias" does little to explain either the celebratory acclaim of 1980 or the critical edge of 1993. No more can "bias" explain why most religion stories take the form they do. What is needed, instead, are more discerning categories—ones that place religion coverage within the context of American history and culture.

NOTES

1. *Atlanta Journal,* March 16, 1896.
2. Direct mail from the National Right to Life Committee, Washington,

D.C., 1990. Quoted in James Davison Hunter, *Culture Wars: The Struggle to Define America* (New York: Basic Books, 1991), 227.

3. Robert S. Lynd and Helen Merrell Lynd, *Middletown: A Study in American Culture* (New York: Harcourt, Brace, 1929), 407, 530-31, 534.

4. Hornell Hart, "Changing Social Attitudes and Interests," in *Recent Social Trends in the United States* (New York: McGraw Hill, 1933), 412; Hornell Hart, "Religion," *American Journal of Sociology* 47 (July 1941-May 1942): 893.

5. Robert B. Pettit, "Religion through the Times: An Examination of the Secularization Thesis through Content Analysis of the New York Times, 1855-1975," unpublished Ph.D. diss., Columbia University, 1986, 253, 301-9.

6. Kenneth Dayton Nordin, "Consensus Religion: National Newspaper Coverage of Religious Life in America, 1849-1960," unpublished Ph.D. diss., University of Michigan, 1975, 81-83. It is worth noting that nineteenth-century newspapers had many fewer pages, and many more stories on the front page, then newspapers now have.

7. *Editor and Publisher,* July 5, 1958, 43.

8. H. Wesley Perkins, "Research Note: Religious Content in American, British, and Canadian Popular Publications from 1937 to 1979," *Sociological Analysis* 45, no. 2 (1984): 164.

9. Glenn Himebaugh and Scott Arnold, "'We Now Cover Faith, Not Bazaars,'" *Bulletin of the American Society of Newspaper Editors* (October 1982): 26.

10. Stewart Hoover, Barbara M. Hanley, and Martin Radelfinger, *The RNS-Lilly Study of Religion Reporting and Readership in the Daily Press* (Philadelphia: Temple University School of Communications and Theater, 1989), 8.

11. Ari Goldman, *The Search for God at Harvard* (New York: Random House, 1991), 198-99.

12. See Tina Rosenberg, "How the Media Made the Moral Majority," *Washington Monthly* 14 (May 1982): 26-34.

13. Andrew M. Greeley, *Unsecular Man: The Persistence of Religion* (New York: Schocken Books, 1972), 7.

14. Pettit, "Religion through the Times," 119.

15. S. Robert Lichter and Stanley Rothman, "Media and Business Elites," *Public Opinion* 4 (October-November 1981): 42-43. The study was, with Linda S. Lichter added as coauthor, expanded to book length as *The Media Elite* (Bethesda: Adler and Adler, 1986).

16. Jerry Falwell, "Morality and the Press," *Fundamentalist Journal* 2 (October 1983): 8.

17. Richard John Neuhaus, *The Naked Public Square: Religion and Democracy in America* (Grand Rapids: William B. Eerdmans, 1984), 99.

18. Garry Wills, *Under God: Religion and American Politics* (New York: Simon and Schuster, 1990), 18.

19. Michael Medved, *Hollywood vs. America: Popular Culture and the War on Traditional Values* (New York: HarperCollins Publishers, 1992), 64–65.

20. Stephen L. Carter, *The Culture of Disbelief* (New York: Basic Books, 1993), 59–60.

21. B. Bruce-Briggs traces the neoconservative polemical assault on the New Class to three articles by Daniel Patrick Moynihan, Norman Podhoretz, and Irving Kristol that appeared in 1972. B. Bruce-Briggs, "An Introduction to the Idea of the New Class," in B. Bruce-Briggs, ed., *The New Class?* (New Brunswick: Transaction Books, 1979), 1–5. In the same volume, Peter Berger argues that the New Class is a "highly secularized part of the American population," although he admits that "my arguments are based on a relative paucity of controlled data and are, in principle, subject to modification as more data appear." Berger, "The Worldview of the New Class," 50.

22. William Fodiak, "How the Catholic Clergy in Pennsylvania Views the Media," *Editor and Publisher*, December 27, 1986, 40.

23. Hoover, Hanley, and Radelfinger, *The RNS–Lilly Study*, 30.

24. John Dart and Jimmy Allen, *Bridging the Gap: Religion and the News Media* (Nashville: Freedom Forum First Amendment Center, 1993), 35–37.

25. J. Daniel Hess, "The Religious Journals' Image of the Mass Media," *Journalism Quarterly* 41 (Winter 1964): 107.

26. *Christianity Today*, April 9, 1971, 36.

27. David H. Weaver and G. Cleveland Wilhoit, *The American Journalist: A Portrait of U.S. News People and Their Work* (Bloomington: Indiana University Press, 1986), 24–25.

28. Dart and Allen, *Bridging the Gap*, 37, 35.

29. Judith Buddenbaum, "Religion News Coverage in Three Major Newspapers," *Journalism Quarterly* 63 (Autumn 1986): 605.

30. Tim Graham and Steve Kaminski, "Faith in a Box: The Network News on Religion, 1993," *News Report No. 4* (Alexandria: Media Research Center, 1994).

31. *Religious News Service*, December 29, 1993; Judith Buddenbaum, "Religion News Coverage in Network Newscasts," in *Religious Television: Controversies and Conclusions*, ed. Robert Abelman and Stewart Hoover (Norwood: Ablex Publishing, 1990), 249–63; and "Network News Coverage of Religion," in *Channels of Belief: Religion and American Commercial Television*, ed. John P. Ferre (Ames: Iowa State University Press, 1990), 57–77.

32. S. Robert Lichter, Daniel Amundson, and Linda S. Lichter, *Media Coverage of the Catholic Church* (N.p: The Center for Media and Public Affairs, 1991), 8.

33. *Commonweal*, May 17, 1991, 307–9, June 14, 1991, 414–15. For a more positive assessment of the study by a Catholic periodical, see *America*, April 20, 1991, 436–37.

34. Garry Wills, "The Greatest Story Ever Told," *Columbia Journalism Review* 19 (January-February 1980): 25–33. For a more generous perspective on papal visits as celebratory media events, see Daniel Dayan, Elihu Katz, and Paul Kerns, "Armchair Pilgrimages: The Trips of John Paul II and Their Television Public — An Anthropological View," *Mass Communication Review Yearbook* 5 (Beverly Hills: Sage Publications, 1985), 227–38.

35. Religious News Service, August 26, 1993.

36. New York Times News Service, August 20, 1993.

Part 2

Spiritual Topics

CHAPTER FOUR

Topoi in
the News

Students of journalism have often noted the stereotypical character
of news stories. "The content may change, but the forms will be enduring," writes Paul Rock. "Much news is, in fact, ritual. It conveys
an impression of endlessly repeated drama whose themes are familiar and well-understood."[1] Working journalists themselves recognize
how limited their repertoire is. "There are twelve stories in the big
city," goes a traditional newsroom joke. "And we're going to tell them
over and over and over again." An even more reductive scheme, noted
by Martin Mayer, claims that only two real stories exist in journalism:
naming the guilty parties and identifying the defective parts.[2]

In an engaging account of his early career as a newspaper reporter,
the historian Robert Darnton explains this narrative stereotyping by
way of a *graffito* he once observed on the wall of a *New York Times*
men's room: "All the News That Fits We Print." "The writer meant
that one can only get articles into the paper if there is enough space
for them, but he might have been expressing a deeper truth: newspaper stories must fit cultural preconceptions of news. Yet 8 million
people live out their lives every day in New York City, and I felt overwhelmed by the disparity between their experience, whatever it was,
and the tales that they read in the *Times*."[3] Unlike many critics of
the media, Darnton does not accuse newsfolk of distorting reality to
suit their own sovereign prejudices. He understands, as only a practitioner fully can, that the cultural preconceptions found in reporting

are stock sentiments and figures that journalists share with their public—and from which they learn not to deviate too far.[4]

Consider a minor reportorial subgenre: the academic meeting story.
By convention, a journalistic account of the annual meeting of the
Modern Language Association (or the American Academy of Religion) begins by reciting a few amusing and/or arcane-sounding paper
titles the reporter has culled from the program of events. This opening tells readers they are now in the presence of that stock figure, the
egghead, who as usual is preoccupied with things the rest of us find
either incomprehensible or silly; and the article generally continues in
a jocular, mildly anti-intellectual vein. The implicit characterization of
the American intellectual as a person not to be taken too seriously—
comfortable to journalist and reader alike—supplies the story with a
familiar (social) context of meaning.[5]

In classical forensic rhetoric, general conceptions of this sort were
literally called commonplaces—*koinoi topoi* in Greek, *loci communes*
in Latin. The orator, as part of his craft, would work up set pieces
on a range of topoi that could then be dropped into a speech to amplify and strengthen the particular case he was arguing.[6] Expressing
judgments about some aspect of human nature, behavior, social institutions, or public policy, these "simple and uncomplicated themes of
a general character" were, to the first-century rhetorician Quintilian,
essential for winning cases.

> What does it matter whether we have to decide whether Milo
> was justified in killing Clodius, or whether it is justifiable to kill
> a man who has set an ambush for his slayer, or a citizen whose
> existence is a danger to the state, even though he has set no such
> ambush? What difference is there between the question whether
> it was an honourable act on the part of Cato to make over Marcia
> to Hortensius or whether such an action is becoming to a virtu-
> ous man? It is on the guilt or innocence of specific persons that
> judgement is given, but it is on general principles that the case
> ultimately rests.[7]

Anyone who has heard closing arguments in criminal cases knows
that lawyers still rely on topoi: "Young people do not understand the
consequences of their acts and should therefore not be punished too
severely," says counsel for the defense. "The trouble with society today
is that young people are taught they can get away with murder," re-

sponds the prosecutor. As Cicero suggested, the contest between defense and prosecution entails a battle of conflicting topoi.[8]

Just as topoi offer jurors moral principles for rendering judgment, so they provide the focus (indeed, the rationale) for journalistic narratives. To be sure, the topoi in news reporting are usually implicit; making them explicit is the homiletic business of editorial writers, columnists, and talk-show hosts. Yet on occasion even a straight news story will declare its topos outright.

> A 17-year-old Long Island girl delivered a full-term baby boy in the bathroom of her parents' home on Tuesday, stuffed him in a plastic bag and then left him in a neighbor's trash can where he was found dead, the Nassau County police said today.
>
> The case reflected the tragic consequences of teen-age pregnancy, with medical officials saying that the girl, Roxana Ramos of Manorhaven, should have received counseling and prenatal care, and in fact, would have been eligible for it under Medicaid.

"The tragic consequences of teen-age pregnancy": Here is the age-old topos of fallen maidenhood, although where once upon a time the narrative might have turned on the false promises of a disappeared lover, this 1993 *New York Times* story points out, sociologically, that the young woman had fallen in with the wrong crowd—"the hoods." And where once religion might have been proffered as the means for averting the tragedy, now it is professional medical help (available at state expense).[9]

In his classic study *European Literature and the Latin Middle Ages,* Ernst Robert Curtius used the concept of the topos to trace the evolution of ancient literary forms during the Middle Ages. By showing how old formulas and conventions were transformed, and how new ones were created out of whole cloth, Curtius opened a window on the cultural values of medieval society.[10] Similarly, the topoi old and new that are employed in both news accounts and popular fiction, television and the movies, cast light on our own system of values. They represent the moral architecture of society, the design and framework within which public discourse takes place.

The more widely shared the view it expresses, the less noticeable will a topos be. In late-twentieth-century America, few would question the judgment that public officials should not take money from private citizens who wish to receive special consideration; few would

therefore question the legitimacy of a story that exposes a politician
who is on the take. Yet in times and places where the under-the-table
payoff is normal and accepted behavior, the "it is wrong for politicians to be on the take" topos would make little sense to readers.

In any society, the spotlight of moral attention moves, attitudes
evolve, and laws themselves are altered. These changes tend to be accompanied by new or revived journalistic topoi (although whether as
cause or effect may be a matter of debate). In the case of narcotics use,
for example, American press coverage has generally been in step with
a shifting public consensus. Conflicting and uncertain attitudes in the
nineteenth century gave way, in the early twentieth, to an antidrug
consensus that culminated in the passage of the Harrison Narcotic
Act in 1914. The accompanying topos, "drugs are bad," did not begin
to falter until the 1950s, and by the late 1960s marijuana and cocaine
had come to regarded, in the media and in society at large, as relatively benign.[11] But the antidrug topos came back stronger than ever
in the 1980s, as once again a "war on drugs" was declared and editors began assigning stories on the evils of narcotics use—in the inner
city, in Hollywood, wherever. By the early 1990s, arguments favoring
legalization of marijuana or cocaine had become marginalized.[12]

Where broad public consensus is difficult to come by, the topoi
will be more evident as points of view; charges of "media bias" are
then certain to be leveled by those who feel the topoi are stacked
against them. Such is the case with the abortion issue. In *The Press
and Abortion, 1838–1988,* Marvin Olasky offers a detailed account of
the news media's changing moral stance toward abortion from an
anti-abortion perspective. At the outset, he shows, daily newspapers
ignored abortion in their news columns but were happy to accept
a considerable amount of (euphemistically expressed) advertising by
abortionists. By the late nineteenth century, crusading against abortion was on the agenda of moral reform, and several anti-abortion
topoi came to be established: the profiteering abortionist (protected
by corrupt political connections); the danger to the woman's health;
the death of the unborn child; the violation of law. In the twentieth century, the unborn child tended to drop out of abortion stories.
Gradually, the focus of evil shifted from abortion itself to the "unscrupulous" abortionist. Legal abortion, not vigorous enforcement of
anti-abortion laws, became the guarantor of the health of the mother.
Olasky is at pains to point out the inadequacies of the pro-abortion

topoi, assailing the press for failing to pursue stories about alleged un-sanitary conditions in abortion clinics. Leaving aside the question of whether the press is in fact biased in favor of the pro-abortion posi-tion, we may note that Olasky's strategy is to trump the (debated) topos that abortion should be a woman's right with a well-nigh in-disputable one: that unsanitary health facilities are bad. As in the courtroom, disagreement over news coverage takes the form of con-flicting topoi.[13]

All in all, the topoi used by the news media are like reflections on a pond, sometimes clear and distinct, sometimes distorted. The distor-tions may result from turbulence in the air or in the pond, but sooner or later, the clarity will reassert itself; the topoi will mirror public atti-tudes, if only because it is in the nature of the media to need to be com-prehensible to the undifferentiated audience it seeks — that is, morally comprehensible, for the media trade largely in tales of good and evil.

What does this mean for representations of religion in a society that has, for two centuries, been distinguished by an incredible variety of often conflicting religious experience and allegiance?

I have elsewhere described religion in America as caught between the twin impulses of conversion (the inclination to see one's own faith as exclusively right) and adhesion (the readiness to recognize all faiths as part of a legitimate tapestry of "American" faith).[14] In its representa-tions of religion, the news media will necessarily be drawn toward the adhesional pole. Understanding only too well that the desired audi-ence professes many faiths, the media can ill afford to draw the circle of acceptable religion too small. At the same time, the majority view may be — indeed, I shall argue, is — a good deal less expansive than the religion clauses of the U.S. Constitution would seem to require. If topoi represent a series of moral least common denominators, it is not obvious, in the case of religion, what those denominators are.

Like other subjects for journalistic attention, religion has its famil-iar story types. In 1993, the senior religion writer for the *New York Times*, Peter Steinfels, sketched a list of Basic Religion Stories as fol-lows:

- Religious leader reveals feet of clay (or turns out to be scoundrel).
- Ancient faith struggles to adjust to modern times.
- Scholars challenge long-standing beliefs.

- Interfaith harmony overcomes inherited enmity.
- New translation of sacred scripture sounds funny.
- Devoted members of a zealous religious group turn out to be warm, ordinary folks.

In Steinfel's view, many of these "pre-existing plot lines . . . ultimately descend from the tension between religious faith and the Eighteenth-Century Enlightenment."[15] The argument here, to the contrary, will be that secular-religious tension is far less important than Western religious culture per se in explaining how the American news media cover religion.

In August 1834 the Rev. J. R. McDowell, publisher of a muckraking religious monthly called *McDowell's Journal,* wrote a spirited defense of his methods, "Shall Licentiousness Be Concealed, or Exposed?" Citing chapter and verse from Jewish and Christian Scriptures, McDowell argued that the Bible both preached and practiced exposure, with respect as much "to the abominations of the *world,* as to those of the *church.*" In this, he wrote, the Bible was at one with the ordinances of secular government: "Those therefore who oppose the detection and exposure of vice, must see that they are acting in opposition to the best interests of society, and to the collective wisdom and experience of legislators in every age of the world. *But this is not all:* Such opposers must find themselves acting in fearful opposition to the Precept and Practice of the Bible, and of the Bible's God."[16] As has been amply demonstrated, this is scarcely the only view of disclosure vouchsafed by the Judeo-Christian tradition. But the prophetic habit of exposing and denouncing vice is not only a fundamental part of Western religion, it is also deeply ingrained in American history, from abolitionism through temperance, women's suffrage, and civil rights. To be sure, even the devil can quote Scripture, although in the late twentieth century there may be crusading editors who are unable to. That does not mean, however, that their zeal for justice, for afflicting the comfortable and comforting the afflicted, came forth in a secular vacuum. Nor does the media's treatment of religion exist apart from the larger culture.

Too often, discussion of religion in the media goes no farther than deciding whether a given account is "positive" or "negative." Religious liberals as well as religious conservatives tend to regard the media as embodying a culture to which they are opposed; it is through the media, after all, that they learn most of what they know of that culture. But such a characterization is far too blunt, self-serving, and parochial to serve as an instrument of analysis. Ignorant of religion, even hostile to it, some news professionals may be; but the images of religion that they put on display reflect something other than their personal ignorance or hostility. When the news media set out to represent religion, they do not approach it from the standpoint of the secular confronting the sacred. They are operating with ideas of what religion is and is not, of what it ought and ought not be—with topoi—that derive, to varying degrees, from religious sources.

The remainder of this book is devoted to an examination of what these topoi are and how they function in journalistic discourse. It is not intended to comprise an exhaustive catalog, as if all religion stories can be subsumed under good works, tolerance, hypocrisy, false prophecy, inclusion, supernatural belief, or declension. Other topoi and sub-topoi are there to be discerned and explored. But these seem to me to be the salient ones, boundary stones that mark out the territory that religion occupies in American journalism. As will be seen, it is territory that American journalists have been treading for a long time, and the American public knows very well how to respond to the tales of sin and salvation, of wonder and woe, that are found on the premises.

NOTES

1. Paul Rock, "News as Eternal Recurrence," in *The Manufacture of News: A Reader,* ed. Stan Cohen and Jock Young (Beverly Hills: Sage Publications, 1973 [73–80]), 77.

2. Martin Mayer, *Making News* (Garden City: Doubleday, 1987).

3. Robert Darnton, "Journalism: All the News That Fits We Print," in *The Kiss of Lamourette* (New York: Norton, 1990), 92 [originally appeared in *Daedalus* (Spring 1975)].

4. Darnton, "Journalism," 88–90.

5. It is an opening ("lede") that probably does not predate the large disciplinary dog-and-pony shows of the post-World War II era; future investigators might do well to search for the *locus classicus* in a *New Yorker* "Talk of the Town" piece from the mid-1950s. How entrenched it has become I discovered when I tried to avoid using it in a story about the 1988 American Sociological Association meeting in Atlanta. The story was fine, said my editor, except for

the lede. Where were the funny paper titles? Needless to say, they were duly inserted.

6. Thus the *Ad C. Herennium,* an anonymous textbook of the first century B.C., specifies ten commonplaces that an orator can use to amplify an argument.

7. Quintilian, *The Institutio Oratoria,* trans. H. E. Butler (Cambridge: Harvard University Press, 1958), vol. 4 (X.v.13), 121.

8. Cicero, *De Inventione,* trans. H. M. Hubbell (Cambridge: Harvard University Press, 1949), 209–13.

9. *New York Times,* June 3, 1993. Curiously enough, the author of the article was the sometime *Times* religion writer Ari Goldman, who would have been capable of smuggling in a religious moral.

10. "But whereas antique topics is part of a didascalium, and hence is systematic and normative, let us try to establish the basis for a historical topics." Ernst Robert Curtius, *European Literature and the Latin Middle Ages,* trans. Willard R. Trask (New York: Pantheon, 1953), 82–83.

11. A shift in press views of LSD from favorable to hostile has been traced by William Braden in "LSD and the Press," in *Psychedelics: The Uses and Abuses of Hallucinogenic Drugs,* ed. Bernard S. Aaronson and Humphrey Osmond (New York: Doubleday, 1970). Why, Braden asks, was there no reporting on "bad trips" in the early, positive coverage? And why did the newspapers have virtually nothing good to say about LSD once the prevailing negative view was established?

12. See H. Wayne Morgan, *Drugs in America: A Social History* (Syracuse: Syracuse University Press, 1981).

13. Marvin Olasky, *The Press and Abortion, 1838–1988* (Hillsdale: Lawrence Erlbaum Associates, 1988), passim.

14. See Mark Silk, *Spiritual Politics: Religion and America* (New York: Simon and Schuster, 1988), 18–22.

15. Peter Steinfels, "Constraints of the Religion Reporter," *Nieman Reports* 47 (Summer 1993): 4.

16. Marvin Olasky, *Central Ideas in the Development of American Journalism: A Narrative History* (Hillsdale: Lawrence Erlbaum Associates, 1991), 15, 153. Appendix D comprises excerpts from McDowell's essay.

CHAPTER FIVE

Good Works

Is not this the fast that I have chosen? to loose the
bands of wickedness, to undo the heavy burdens,
and to let the oppressed go free, and that ye break
every yoke? Is it not to deal thy bread to the hun-
gry, and that thou bring the poor that are cast out
to thy house?

ISAIAH 58:6–7

The American news media presuppose that religion is a good thing.
The church notes, calendars of events, and stories of congregational
goings-on that fill the Saturday religion pages bespeak institutions that
are benefiting their members and the community at large. How can
these institutions, to which the mass media's mass audience belongs,
not be presumed good? Particular religious phenomena will be portrayed as socially harmful or even evil, but these are abuses, misdeeds
done "in the name of" religion. As hostile, ham-handed, or ignorant as their approach may sometimes appear, the media will never be
caught attacking religion as such. Yet what exactly makes it a force for
good in their eyes?

In the fall of 1991, former president Jimmy Carter announced
that he would lead a large, volunteer effort to help the poor neighborhoods of metropolitan Atlanta. Characteristically, Carter cast his
"Atlanta Project" in the form of a prophetic mission, and he did not
shrink from the prophet's critique of institutional religion. Asserting
that "the churches" screen their members off from the real world of
poverty and need, he called them "basically a dormant element of self-
gratification and security."

Several months later, on April 19, 1992, the *Atlanta Journal-Constitution* used this assault as a stalking horse in producing a special eight-page Easter section, "Jimmy Carter's Challenge to Religion," that looked at what Atlanta's religious community was doing for the poor. It was not a hard-hitting report; no effort was made to portray any particular churches or faiths as embodiments of dormant self-gratification. The section did, however, present a generalized portrait of a religious community that was not doing enough, and with it the implicit claim that the proper business of religion is to promote good works.

To support the claim, the newspaper relied on a poll it conducted in which 84 percent of respondents said they believed a religious person has a responsibility to take an active role in helping the poor. Ninety percent of once-a-week worshipers indicated that they felt such an obligation incumbent upon themselves personally. (Somewhat less noteworthy from the newspaper's point of view were the nearly 60 percent of respondents who expressed the view that their own religious organizations were doing about the right amount.)[1] Besides the polling numbers, the section included thumbnail accounts of what an array of religious groupings, including Islam and "Hinduism/Buddhism," teach on the subject of charity. The only group characterized as ambivalent about helping the poor was "Evangelicals," about whom it was said: "Historically fervent spreaders of the Word such as Baptists and Pentecostals often emphasize soul-saving over social ministry. There are signs that may be changing, in favor of a balance between the two approaches." No evidence of such a change was adduced, however; and although Baptists and Pentecostals are legion in metropolitan Atlanta, nowhere could one of them be found denigrating charity in favor of evangelism. In this way, the topos "religion ought to devote itself to helping the poor" took on the aspect of a universal truth.

Why should the newspaper have skated over contrary views on this point? The introduction of authoritative disagreement would have muddied the moral clarity of what was, in effect, an Easter sermon to the community at large. It might also have suggested to readers that the newspaper was presuming to tell "the churches" what to do instead of merely acting as the vox populi. If that meant giving short shrift to the evangelical point of view that historically has predominated in the religious life of the South, so be it.[2]

Consider, by contrast, a *New York Times* article on September 7,

1993 on the gathering of the National Baptist Convention. The claim of the article (announced in the headline, "Black Baptists Focusing on Social Ills") was that the nation's largest black denomination was evolving from "a conservative group whose leadership once disagreed with the tactics of Dr. Martin Luther King Jr. to a more progressive organization that opposed the Persian Gulf war and actively sought to address social ills plaguing blacks." But while suggesting that this "progressive" shift was right and proper, the article took note of internal critics who thought the black church was losing sight of its "primary mission" of helping people find salvation through Jesus. "There are social agencies," the Rev. James Waller of Philadelphia was quoted as saying. "If the church does not spread the gospel, will the lawyer? Will the school teacher?" The *Times,* which was not in this instance preaching to the community as a whole, went ahead in the conventional journalistic manner and quoted the other side.

It is important to recognize the degree to which both this article and the *Journal-Constitution*'s special section embody a moral stance that is derived not from a secular worldview but from the Western religious tradition. The thoroughgoing secularist would argue, as the evangelical Reverend Waller did, that religion should concern itself with belief and devotion and leave social welfare to the state and other nonreligious entities. But in media accounts of religion, the social gospel is alive and well. Good religion helps those afflicted by disaster, whether man-made or heaven-sent.

After the 1992 Los Angeles riots that followed the first Rodney King trial, newspapers across the country ran stories on prayer services designed to encourage their respective communities to, in King's phrase, "get along." On May 19, 1992, the *Boston Globe* had as its lead, front-page story: "Black Clerics in City Issue Proposals for Self-help." Less than a week later, on May 25, another lead story, "Boston Clergy Urge Crusade on Violence," described a letter read from the pulpit by the city's black pastors, to the effect that the riots had persuaded them to expand their mission beyond "the salvation of souls" to include "the salvation of our communities." These stories were given such prominence not only because of Los Angeles but also as the result of a widely publicized attack on mourners during a wake at a Baptist church in the city's black Mattapan district. The newspaper clearly wanted to do what it could to promote the churches' "revived commitment to encourage community responsibility."

During the upper Mississippi flood of 1993, the Religious News Service carried a series of stories about the help churches were providing to the victims. ("Even as the rivers of the Midwest rose, overwhelming their banks, churches and church members in the area and across the nation were themselves rising in response to the disaster.")[3] The stories focused for the most part on the fund-raising efforts of particular denominations and Church World Services, the relief arm of the National Council of Churches. Duly noted was the visit of South Africa's Anglican archbishop Desmond Tutu to a flooding site, where he helped fill a sandbag, as was the call of the Roman Catholic bishop of St. Louis for priests and parishioners to offer prayers, time, and money to help the flood victims.[4]

Religious leaders could also help by plumbing the deeper meaning of a disaster of this sort. Mike Harden of the *Columbus* [Ohio] *Dispatch* found the Rev. Kelly Allen surveying her sandbagged neighborhood in St. Genevieve, Missouri, from the steps of the First Presbyterian Church. Allen talked about how she was trying to "find the presence of God in all this," suggesting that the flood gave the residents of the small town a chance to experience a wider sense of community through what the reporter called "the Samaritan qualities of absolute strangers." Said the pastor: "This kind of suffering is surmountable, and there may even be a redeeming quality about it in the end."[5] Thus does classic Christian theodicy find its way into secular news coverage. But a plague on those who would oppose ministries of succor. Under the headline "Cold Shoulder to Churches That Practice Preachings," a front-page *New York Times* story from March 27, 1994 began, "Never mind the biblical injunctions to feed the poor and shelter the homeless. Increasingly, many Americans do not want the social service programs of religious institutions in their neighborhoods."

More "reportable," more susceptible to evaluation by secular criteria, socially active religion engages the moral attention of the news media in a way that ordinary religious practice cannot. There is nothing very new about this. In 1940, speaking to University of Colorado journalism students, the Denver *Post*'s managing editor Lawrence C. Martin argued that if newspapers were failing to foster religion in the community it was because the churches themselves had created the impression that they were "not only detached from, but actually indifferent to, the problems of the day."

To overcome that impression, the church needs to establish a claim on news space. Here and there a beginning has been made, for churchmen are beginning to grapple with social problems within their own membership. For example, one church in Denver has for some time been operating an employment service to bring together the people of that church who need work and those who have work to offer. This service has worked so well that it is now being expanded to cover the whole city, and in due time that will be a news item. Another church group has undertaken a practical study of relief, which today in Denver is a pressing and dangerous problem. These are small beginnings, but they are beginning to receive attention in the press.[6]

According to Kenneth Nordin, the proportion of front-page religion stories relating to the amelioration of society rose steadily from 25 percent in 1849 to 63 percent in 1960.[7] It is probably not too much to say that during that time the press came to see involvement in social reform as the most important reason for covering religion.

Occasionally, a newspaper may attempt what the *Boston Globe* did in the summer of 1993. Using its summer interns to gather the evidence, the newspaper fashioned an extensive front-page package showing the variety of Bostonians' spiritual experiences. ("People pray to Allah, Buddha, Krishna, Jehovah and Jesus Christ.") The inevitable opinion poll found that religion was "very" or "somewhat" important to 73 percent of respondents. A testament to religious pluralism and adherence, the story on August 15 (headlined "Solace, Unity Found in Tapestry of Religions") suggested that, no matter what the faith, the spiritual benefits were the same. *E pluribus unum.*

It is the religious calendar that gives ordinary religion its greatest salience, as the media take their annual notice of Christmas and Easter; of Rosh Hashana, Yom Kippur, Hanukkah, and Passover; and increasingly of non-Judeo-Christian festivals like Ramadan.[8] Photos of Christmas trees and Santas, of bright children's faces before a Menorah, touching and monitory stories of the season — these are the despair of journalists condemned to render up this year what they rendered the year before. The stories are known in the trade as "evergreens," foliage that seems to last forever.

Over the long sweep of time, the evergreens do change. In the earlier part of the century, newspapers filled their pages with portraits and accounts of young women in their Easter finery and covered the Easter parade as a major cultural event. Today, the Easter season, far less important socially (and economically), is more likely to be marked by a prominently displayed article on the status of religion (often imperiled in some way). The Christmas offerings nowadays comprise not only tales of good cheer and good works, but also reminders that 'tis the season of psychological distress. Still, the journalistic traditions are hard to break. Since 1911, the *New York Times* has mounted an annual charity drive between Thanksgiving and Christmas. In earlier decades, page upon page of the *Times* would be taken up with short accounts of the hundred "neediest cases." More recently, these have been winnowed down to a dozen or so exemplary tales, buttressed by aggregate statistics and accounts of hard-pressed social welfare agencies.[9] This has, to some extent, dissipated the pleasant illusion of *Times* reporters scouring Gotham for the worthiest recipients of readers' charity. For all that, the newspaper's philanthropic formula has remained essentially intact for the better part of a century.

In general, however, the dutiful conventions of the news media deliver the seasonal merchandise less effectively than popular entertainment does. Christmas movies, the premiere morality tales of twentieth-century America, are a study in themselves. Without attempting that here, it is worth drawing attention, in an era of talk about traditional family values, to one of the genre's recurrent topoi, the good work of safeguarding bourgeois domesticity.

In *Christmas in Connecticut*, a 1945 Warner Brothers release, Barbara Stanwyck portrays a single Manhattanite magazine writer who has wowed the nation with a homemaking column about her blissful life on an exurban farm. When her straitlaced publisher (Sidney Greenstreet) decides to visit her for Christmas, she must simulate the domestic existence she writes about. ("Millions of women in these United States pattern their daily lives after that feature. And you're going to live up to their ideals or I'm not Alexander Yardley.") A sailor recovering from a war injury also turns up at the Connecticut farmstead for the holiday, and, after much comic byplay, he and Stanwyck fall in love. In proper postwar fashion, she ends up abandoning her career for the domestic ideal she fabricated in order to preserve it.

A half-century later, the 1993 Christmas season featured *Mrs. Doubtfire*, a film in which the professional woman is played by Sally Fields. In the film's opening scenes, Fields's marriage breaks up, the victim of her career-mindedness and the fecklessness of her out-of-work actor-husband, Robin Williams. Incapable of being deprived of daily contact with his three children, Williams tricks himself out as the very incarnation of domestic virtuosity, a British housekeeper, and is hired by Fields. As the redoubtable Mrs. Doubtfire, he shapes up the children, wards off Fields's new boyfriend, and in the process gets his own domestic act together. This is the nineties, and all Williams definitively gets for his pains are visitation rights every afternoon. But the loving smiles of his ex strongly suggest a full-dress reconciliation. Meanwhile, kids everywhere are assured that, no matter how many live-in parents they have, "You'll have a family in your heart forever."

For the most concrete symbolization of this topos there is *Home Alone*, in which an American family commits the ultimate holiday sacrilege of leaving its snow-bedecked suburban colonial to celebrate Christmas in, of all places, Paris, France. The ne'er-do-well eight-year-old, left behind by accident, ends up having to defend the hearth against two comic burglars with the distinctly non-Christian names of Marv and Harry. In the end, the family returns, reunited on Christmas day in the place they should never have left in the first place. As Dorothy chants as she wishes herself back from fairy-tale Oz to her depression-battered Kansas farm, "There's no place like home."[10]

A small gag in *Home Alone* shows the vacationing family sitting in a Parisian hotel room and watching a French-dubbed version of *It's a Wonderful Life*, the apotheosis of Hollywood domestic fables. The life in question belongs to a hero of the American home: the owner of a "building and loan" savings bank, he enables families of modest means to realize the American dream of homeownership. But James Stewart is depressed that this calling has prevented him from ever leaving his provincial hometown, and he is about to lose the bank to the evil Lionel Barrymore. Attempting suicide, he is rescued by a bumbling guardian angel and given the "second chance" of a trip through the hell of a community that has been deprived of his existence. The experience persuades him that his life has indeed been wonderful, and he is restored to the bosom of his family under the aegis of the Christmas tree, the evergreen lares and penates that preside over the well-being of the American home.[11]

But all this is Hollywood. Journalists live in a world where heartwarming fables of moral uplift are harder to come by, or at least harder to spin into gold. For better or worse, it comes more naturally to the news media to define good religion by a *via negativa* through recounting tales of intolerance, hypocrisy, false prophecy, and spiritual decline.

NOTES

1. A third felt their organizations were not doing enough, as compared with 3 percent who believed they was doing too much.

2. The opening paragraphs of the *Journal-Constitution*'s lead Easter Sunday editorial did offer something of the sort:

> In charging Atlanta's churches with being "a dormant element of self-gratification and security," former President Jimmy Carter has issued a challenge to churchgoers that harks back to the Hebrew prophets. Of these predecessors, none was more eloquent than Isaiah prophesying that what God truly requires of us by way of repentance is not sackcloth and ashes but "to deal thy bread to the hungry, and that thou bring the poor that are cast out to thy house."
>
> But charity is not a simple issue in the Christian tradition. In Matthew, Jesus defends a woman who pours precious ointment on his head against the criticism of his disciples, who felt the ointment should have been sold and the money given to the poor: "For ye have the poor always with you; but me ye have not always."
>
> The relationship between faith and works has exercised theologians since Paul, and different Christian denominations have evolved different views. In twelfth-century Catholicism, there was vigorous debate over whether good works were to be done for the sake of one's neighbor, or simply for the sake of one's own soul.
>
> Liberal Christians argue today that charity should be given without pushing one's faith on the recipients. Conservative evangelicals hold that the greatest good work that can be done for anyone is to expose him to the Gospel.
>
> Nevertheless, the vast majority of Atlantans — Christians, Jews, Muslims and others — are agreed that a religious person has a responsibility to take an active role in helping the poor. From today's special section on church giving, it is clear that while much is being done, the glass of benevolence is far from overflowing.

The editorial, which I wrote, was intended to acknowledge the legitimacy of alternatives to the good-works topos of the special section, while still using the results of the opinion poll to urge the churches to support Carter's project.

3. *Religious News Service*, July 13, 1993.

4. *Religious News Service*, July 13, 14, 16, 19, August 6, September 30, 1993. Similar stories were run in the wake of the 1994 California earthquake (RNS, January 18, 19, 20, 26).

5. Reprinted in the *Atlanta Journal-Constitution*, July 26, 1993.

6. "Shop Talk at Thirty," *Editor and Publisher,* April 27, 1940, 106.

7. Kenneth Dayton Nordin, "Consensus Religion: National Newspaper Coverage of Religious Life in America, 1849–1960," unpublished Ph.D. diss., University of Michigan, 1975, 90.

8. Kwanzaa, invented in the 1960s, has achieved similar status in the media as the annual festival of African-American ethnicity.

9. See, for example, the *Times*'s Thanksgiving Day story inaugurating the 1993 "neediest" fund drive, November 25, 1993.

10. *Home Alone II,* unable to repeat an identical assault on the suburban Chicago home, transposes the action to New York City, where it latches onto the closely related myth of downtown Christmas shopping (to buy the presents for domestic gift-giving), by way of a fabulous toy store that the unrepentant Marv and Harry seek to rob.

11. In *Home Alone II,* the mother realizes that her lost son will find his way to the Christmas tree in Rockefeller Center.

CHAPTER SIX

Tolerance

Ye have heard that it hath been said, Thou shalt
love thy neighbour, and hate thine enemy. But I say
unto you, Love your enemies. . . .
MATTHEW 5:43–44

"Separation of church and state" is the shibboleth traditionally used
to identify the complicated intercourse between religion and government in the United States. But in journalistic practice, "separation"
carries too many partisan meanings, and is too tied to ill-understood
and shifting judicial interpretations of constitutional language, to provide clear moral definition for most stories about church and state.
The salient church-state topos has to do, instead, with the virtue of
toleration and the vice of intolerance.

Tolerance, of course, can be considered as merely an expression of
secularist indifference or the desire not to offend. For the mass media,
it makes good business sense to shrink from drawing invidious religious distinctions among the public at large. But as the above passage from the Sermon on the Mount makes plain, tolerance is also a
powerful message in the Western religious tradition.[1] In America, the
Baptist founder of Rhode Island, Roger Williams, instituted the first
regime of complete religious tolerance because he believed that anything less was a transgression against God. In a study conducted in the
1960s, Gordon Allport and Michael Ross found that while Americans
who went to church tended to be more prejudiced than those who did
not, prejudice decreased among those church-goers with greater religious commitment.[2] Though sometimes honored in the breach, the
principle of noninterference in others' freedom of worship has from

the beginning of the republic been central to Americans' self-image. When employing the topos of religious tolerance, the media know this to be a well-nigh unassailable point of view in American public discourse—albeit disputes may arise in a political setting over which side is "truly" tolerant.

In the 1928 and 1960 presidential elections, religious opponents of Governor Al Smith of New York and Senator John F. Kennedy of Massachusetts argued that it would violate the separation of church and state to elect a Roman Catholic president. A Catholic, they said, would take orders from his church, which was doctrinally on record preferring a Roman Catholic polity to church-state separation. Yet once Smith and Kennedy had declared their independence from Roman rule, the press dismissed this ancient and widespread American prejudice.

Smith's initial declaration came in response to an open letter from a New York lawyer in the April 1927 number of the *Atlantic* magazine, which asserted that there was an "irrepressible conflict" between the U.S. Constitution and the claims of the Roman Catholic church and asked Smith whose authority he would obey if elected president. Responding in the magazine's next issue, Smith said he recognized no power in his church to interfere with the Constitution. The statement was greeted with widespread approval, including by newspapers that would not end up supporting Smith, such as the Republican New York *Herald Tribune*.[3] The *Herald Tribune*'s lead story on April 19 reported that "religious and political leaders throughout the country joined yesterday in acclaiming Governor Smith's reply" but noted the belief in political circles that it "had by no means laid the ghost of religious controversy." An editorial the same day underscored the approval, calling Smith's reply "a refreshing statement of sound Americanism that will give the bigots of every church pause," and saying it "may well prove to be a landmark in the history of American tolerance." Similar sentiments were expressed the same day in the heart of the Bible Belt by the Dallas *News*.

Coverage of the election came to characterize the activity of Smith's religious opponents as "the whispering campaign," an expression that carried its own weight of moral disapproval. Not that all of them were whispering. On September 20, Smith made an impassioned speech in Oklahoma City in which he denounced religious opposition to his candidacy as bigotry and charged the Republican National Committee with helping to stir it up. In response, the most that anti-Smith newspapers like the *Herald Tribune* and the *Los Angeles Times* could do was accuse him of exploiting the religious issue for his own benefit. "To attempt, as Governor Smith is doing, to manufacture political capital out of such a situation is hostile to the cause of true tolerance," editorialized the *Herald Tribune* on September 22. Three days later, the newspaper published a cartoon showing two gossips labeled "Religious Intolerance" and "Church Fanaticism" whispering to Uncle Sam as he works at his desk. The caption reads: "There Are Too Many Important Issues to Think About." Overall, as Donald Frederick Brod put it in an examination of press coverage of religion in the campaign, newspapers supporting Hoover "attempted to ignore Smith's religion as much as possible while the Smith supporters kept the issue before the public and depicted Smith as the heroic victim of bigotry."[4] To newspapers of both stripes, the mass of anti-Catholic propaganda that circulated around the country was *non grata*.

In 1960, the press was, if anything, more hostile to anti-Catholicism than thirty-two years before. It was to be expected that Kennedy would win widespread praise for saying to a gathering of ministers in Houston: "I believe in an America where the separation of church and state is absolute — where no Catholic prelate would tell the president (should he be a Catholic) how to act, and no Protestant minister would tell his parishioners for whom to vote." But this time around, the *Herald Tribune* — still Republican and now supporting Richard Nixon — refrained from accusing the Massachusetts senator of capitalizing on the issue.[5] The newspaper also took an active hand in combating what was now called "the underground campaign." In a lead Sunday editorial on September 18, it praised Protestant clergy who forswore opposing Kennedy on religious grounds, and in an October 16 article warned of a "massive new religious attack" on Kennedy's candidacy by the National Association of Evangelicals as well as "some of the main professional propaganda mills" and "hate groups . . . on the gutter level." Brod's assessment is that the press as a whole played a significant role in helping to "erase" anti-Catholic bigotry in the 1960 election.[6]

If the press was able to do more for Kennedy than Smith, it was in part because the religious issue was more nakedly one of anti-Catholic prejudice in 1960. In 1928, Smith campaigned on a platform that called for the repeal of Prohibition, and groups of Protestants declared their opposition to him on that basis. After World War II, the outstanding political issues between Catholics and Protestants concerned public aid to parochial schools and the appointment of an ambassador to the Vatican; but in both cases, Kennedy took the opposite side from his church, thereby hindering anti-Catholicism from masquerading as a concern about policy issues. In the final analysis, opposing a candidate because of his faith seemed un-American, the moral equivalent of violating the Constitution's ban on religious tests for office.

It is worth emphasizing that although the "Temperance" opposition to Smith in 1928 was often denounced as a transparent cover for anti-Catholicism (even that bastion of Republicanism, the *Chicago Tribune*, criticized a Justice Department official for appealing to religious prejudices in the name of Prohibition)[7] there was not the slightest suggestion in the press that it was out of constitutional order for churches to involve themselves in political questions that engaged their moral concerns. Such involvement has, indeed, been a distinguishing mark of American church activity at least since the days of abolitionism. After some years of relative quiescence in the middle decades of the twentieth century, politically active religion again made strong appearances in both the civil rights movement and the movement against the war in Vietnam, not without the approbation of the media. As James Reston wrote in the *New York Times* on August 30, 1963, in the wake of March on Washington, "The first significant test of the Negro march on Washington will come in the churches and synagogues of the country this weekend. . . . as moral principles preceded and inspired political principles in this country, as the church preceded the Congress, so there will have to be a moral revulsion to the humiliation of the Negro before there can be significant political relief."

After what was immediately christened the Christian Right burst upon the scene in the 1980 presidential campaign, it became common to accuse liberals, and the "liberal media," of maintaining a double standard on religion in politics, supporting it in liberal causes but crying violation of church-state separation when it reared its head on the conservative side.[8] Whatever the validity of this charge against liberals in general — and the evidence appears to be largely impressionistic — it is simply untrue when it comes to the allegedly liberal media. To be sure, there was plenty of editorial opposition to what the Christian

Right stood for, but that was hardly equivalent to a denial of its right
to participate in the political process. In fact, the bastions of media
liberalism have consistently expressed support for that right.

From the very first, leaders of the Christian Right, such as the Rev.
Jerry Falwell, took pleasure in pointing out that they were doing no
more than religious liberals had done in supporting the civil rights
and antiwar movements. In an October 13, 1980, story in *Time* magazine, Falwell charged his critics with hypocrisy, saying, "Nobody ever
criticized Martin Luther King when he was using the churches for
political activity. No one has ever criticized the National Council of
Churches and its leaders for 50 years of active political involvement.
What bothers our critics is that we don't agree with them."[9]

But before this criticism even saw the light of day, the religion writer
for the *New York Times,* Kenneth Briggs, had weighed in on October 3,
1980 with an article quoting constitutional experts in support of the
rights of religious activists to engage in politics. "The tradition of the
intermixture of religion and politics is too ingrained in our national
life to be eliminated," said Laurence Tribe, the quintessentially liberal
Harvard law professor. "It is extremely important to the principle of
freedom of speech that this process not stop just because some are dis-
tressed by the content of the speech or the speaker." On October 5, a
Times editorial made exactly the same point. "Liberals further confuse
the matter when they applaud the political passions of, say, Martin
Luther King, but denounce Jerry Falwell's as illegal. The 'wall' that
Jefferson envisioned between church and state will not stand if conceived as a barrier to political speech by religious sects." The *Times* did
draw the line against church endorsements of political candidates—
a line often ignored by the Christian Right—and concluded with the
thought that the real menace comes when people "aim to make religious dogma binding upon others."[10]

In the wake of the 1980 election, as Jerry Falwell and company
basked in some notable electoral successes, Briggs presented the case
as essentially closed:

Many liberals were initially offended simply by the political slant
of the conservatives and tended to suggest that Mr. Falwell and
others were somehow violating the constitutional guarantee of
separation of church and state. But the arguments shifted away
from legalities toward the far more enduring issues of the cor-

rect way to construct a "Christian" outlook on moral and political issues. While they now concede that the conservatives have a right to try to influence the elections, they disagree with the presuppositions behind the activism.[11]

This formulation of the issue reappeared in the same terms in the liberal press during the 1984 campaign—with perhaps greater acknowledgment of the right of the religiously committed to engage in politics. When, at summer's end, the Reagan campaign sent out signals that it had emphasized religion enough, the *Washington Post* editorialized on September 2: "We see no reason for anyone to fall silent on the subject now just because Reagan strategists are having a case of nerves." Noting that religious involvement in politics was long-standing, the *Post* took aim, rather, at the danger of "identifying your cause with a particular set of beliefs," and thus alienating many voters who don't share those beliefs. Likewise, on September 9, the *New York Times* observed:

Intolerance: that's the word that's burning beneath all the smoke about religion and politics, a coupling that offends neither church nor state. There's plenty of religion in politics— and ought to be. People in a democracy should act on their social values, whether derived from their religious faith or from secular sources . . . .

The danger comes from people who are oh so sure they're right, who insist that they alone represent the one true political faith, who revile the other side as godless, intolerant obstructionists.

And, in a package of stories on "Religion and the Pulpit," *Newsweek* asserted that the "absolutism" of John Kennedy in his 1960 Houston address had "raised the wall of church-state separation to unrealistic heights." Not only was the Christian Right on the march, said the magazine, but candidate Jesse Jackson had the black church behind him, and the Catholic bishops were also making their presence felt on the hustings, above all in the matter of abortion. Religion and politics drew on the same "ethical imperatives," and "no arbitrary dividing line can ever completely separate religious beliefs from political passions." Neither Ronald Reagan nor "his court prophets have any intention of fostering a Christian theocracy." But there was a need for

"responsible" religious leaders to formulate a moral language acceptable to secular and religious alike.[12]

By the late 1980s, liberal pundits had become positively blithe about
the prevalence of religion in the political arena. On the eve of the 1988
campaign, for example, the *Washington Post*'s David Broder smiled
benignly on the candidacies of "the two reverends"—Jesse Jackson
and Pat Robertson—as well as on the "new moral and religious commentary" on politics coming from various other ministers. "It's a
healthy phenomenon, in the eyes of this secular reporter-critic, and
not the menace some see," Broder wrote on December 23, 1987. "The
clerics often speak uncomfortable truths to the mighty." After Robertson finished second in the Iowa caucuses (but before he was knocked
for a loop in the South), there may have been a moment of panic,
as noted by James Wall in a March 2, 1988, editorial in the *Christian
Century*: "Is fear of a religious sensibility a strong part of American
political life? In view of the aggressiveness with which the media are
attacking Robertson, it would seem that that fear prevails in at least
some centers of our culture."[13]

Equanimity swiftly returned, however, and by 1989 there was Mark
Shields, the all-purpose Democrat of television punditry, playing
"gotcha" à la Jerry Falwell with the *New York Times*. In that off-year's
election season, the *Times* had criticized San Diego Bishop Leo Maher
for threatening "the truce of tolerance by which Americans maintain
civility and enlarge religious liberty" when he denied communion to
Lucy Killea, a California state assemblywoman running for state senate
who favored abortion rights. Shields pointed out that back in 1962
the *Times* had applauded New Orleans Archbishop Joseph Francis
Rummel for excommunicating Louisiana's white supremacist political boss Leander Perez, who publicly opposed the archbishop's deseg-
regation of diocesan schools. In both cases, said Shields, the church
took ecclesiastical action against a public figure who disagreed with
its moral teachings. (In point of fact, Perez, unlike Killea, had directly
challenged the archbishop's authority.) For interested parties like the
Times, the issue at hand was not any principle of church-state separation but simply whether the clergy "was enlightened enough to agree
with us."[14]

Media acceptance of politics as a religious free-for-all might have
come less readily had not the Christian Right worked so hard to
portray itself as an ecumenical alliance, a "majority" whose morality

was formed by the Judeo-Christian tradition. The other side was thus not other religions, but secularism (or secular humanism) and its loose-living minions—a much easier mark. The tide did eventually seem to turn, however, and the precise moment may have been May 1992 when, in a speech on "traditional values," Vice President Dan Quayle denounced the out-of-wedlock pregnancy of the fictional television newswoman Murphy Brown. That popular character, played by Candice Bergen, was a singularly poor choice of villains, but for the vice president she seemed the enemy incarnate, and he refused to let the matter drop. In June, he told the annual meeting of the Southern Baptist Convention that to stand up for "traditional" values was to invite mockery and ridicule in the nation's newsrooms and television studios, but said he wore the "scorn of the media elite" as a "badge of honor." The reaction to his earlier speech proved, he said, that the "real intolerance was on the other side." [15]

The Murphy Brown episode set the stage for the 1992 Republican national convention, which persuaded much of the general public that the GOP's twelve-year alliance with the Christian Right had gone too far. Using the hard-shell address of conservative pundit and would be presidential nominee Pat Buchanan as a touchstone, news accounts of the cultural politics of the subsequent campaign revolved around the topos of tolerance/intolerance. It was not that the Republicans had transgressed against the separation of church and state, but that their vision of America seemed to exclude so many Americans. "Republican leaders reopened what could be a four-year battle over abortion Friday as party regulars launched a campaign to shake a legacy of the 1992 campaign: the image of intolerance," wrote the *Atlanta-Journal Constitution*'s chief political correspondent on January 30, 1993. Behind the image lay the reality. In the words of outgoing party chair Rich Bond, "Our job is to win elections, not cling to intolerances that zealots call principles."

Tolerance/intolerance is the preferred journalistic topos not only in politics but also in the church-state issues that play themselves out in the courts. The Scopes trial, which in July 1925 turned Dayton, Tennessee, into the greatest church-state media circus in American history, found the press indicting Tennessee in general and William Jennings Bryan in particular for classic religious oppression—as a lead story in the *Atlanta Constitution* put it on July 10, "The greatest battle of the mind since Galileo was imprisoned by the inquisition for teaching the earth is round." Yet the press took pains to present the case not as "religion" versus "science," but as the imposition of narrow religious dogmatism on the population at large. Considerable attention was paid to a Methodist minister in Dayton who quit his pastorate when his congregation protested his decision to let a modernist minister from New York preach. As the *Chicago Tribune* editorialized, also on July 10, "This is a country of many religions. It frequently is referred to in general terms as a Christian nation. In one faith or another the great preponderance of belief is Christian. But is it Mr. Bryan's present opinion that it is the duty of the state by statute to support his definition of the Christian religion as the religion of the state?" Short shrift was given to Bryan's argument that taxpayers should not have to pay for their children to be taught abhorrent doctrines.

An interesting example of the topos in action involves the Christian populist orator and propagandist Gerald L. K. Smith. A leading supporter of Louisiana Governor Huey Long during the depression, in the 1940s Smith became America's most notorious anti-Semite, claiming that World War II had been fought to save the Jews and that the Holocaust was a hoax. Widely assailed in the news media (he won libel actions against *Time, Newsweek,* and the *Wichita Beacon*), he thrived on the publicity and drew large audiences wherever he went. In 1946, one of the country's foremost opponents of anti-Semitism, Rabbi S. A. Fineberg, proposed that the best way to weaken Smith was to persuade the news media not to cover him, and the following year he persuaded the major Jewish organizations to pursue the policy by appealing to the consciences of media leaders and even threatening boycotts of publications, programs, and advertisers. In the event, the silent treatment worked. Stories about Smith moved to the back pages, his audiences dwindled away, and by the early 1950s he had become an insignificant figure on the American scene. There is, perhaps, no better example of the distinction between the topos of tolerance/intolerance and those of free speech and free exercise; or of the media's willingness to scant the latter for the sake of the former.[16]

By the end of the century, a Galileo simile could still be employed from time to time in accounts of, for example, religiously inspired efforts to remove offensive books from local libraries. But after World War II, the church-state cases decided by the U.S. Supreme Court were not easy to fit into a morally compelling story of tolerance and its opposite. Why were Sunday blue laws and subsidized bus rides for parochial school children constitutional but a nondenominational school prayer not? Writing in the wake of the 1962 school prayer decision, the Constitutional scholar Leonard Levy strongly supported the Court's ban but charged the justices with having "failed to prepare the public for a principled decision" because of past inconsistencies.[17]

Editorialists have over the years honed their arguments in support of the legal proscription of school prayers, creches, and other religious "establishments." Such establishments exclude members of minority faiths and those of no faith and represent government intrusion into matters of conscience.[18] But the rationales have not proved convincing to a majority of the population, and, in some school-prayer stories, have taken a back seat to other journalistic topoi. When a school principal in Mississippi was fired for ignoring lawyer's instructions and allowing students to broadcast a morning prayer over the public address system, the main themes were the biracial support in Mississippi for the principal and supporters' belief that school prayer would help alleviate youth violence and generally (in the principal's words) "improve the school climate."[19] Confusion over what constitutes an impermissible establishment of religion could itself become a topos. "Pity the public school principal in December," began a *New York Times* article of December 16, 1993. "Between Hanukkah, Christmas and Kwanzaa, this long last month lays a minefield of grand proportions for educators trying to acknowledge the holidays without bridging the separation of church and state." Indeed, as of 1994, the Supreme Court's religion-clause jurisprudence was sufficiently unsettled that anyone could be forgiven for being confused.

What is clear, however, is that the news media will give much more coverage to establishment-clause issues than to free-exercise claims involving state restrictions on religious practices. This is, quite simply, because there is thought to be, and doubtless is, far more public interest in cases involving "public religion." Doing away with a traditional prayer at high school football games is a big local story. Removing a cross in someone's front yard in deference to a zoning ordinance is not. In 1993, the *Atlanta Journal* plastered a banner headline across its front-page when the Supreme Court permitted access to the public schools by religious groups after hours and let stand a lower-court ruling permitting student-led prayer. But when *Smith v. Employment*

Division effectively gutted the First Amendment's free-exercise clause in 1990, the decision received scant notice, even from the *New York Times.*

In fact, the most undercovered religion story of the early 1990s was the *Smith* decision and the ultimately successful national effort to reverse it by way of the Religious Freedom Restoration Act (RFRA) in 1993. The decision went against two Native Americans in Oregon who sought to obtain unemployment benefits after they were fired from their jobs as drug counselors for using the mind-altering substance peyote in a ceremony of the Native American church. The concern arose not from the rejection of the Native Americans' claims but from the fact that, in so ruling, the Court changed the way it handled all such free-exercise claims. No longer would the government have to demonstrate a "compelling" state interest to get a claim rejected. Any generally applicable law not actually intended to suppress a particular religious practice would henceforth pass constitutional muster.

The law led to the formation of the broadest coalition ever to back a religion bill, extending from the most conservative evangelical groups through mainline denominations and on to the American Civil Liberties Union and People for the American Way. Attempts to reverse Supreme Court decisions in Congress are rare and extraordinary. Even so, the news media took little note. Interesting stories might have been written about the sole religious group opposing the bill, the Roman Catholic bishops, who were persuaded that it might enable a woman to use free-exercise to claim a right to have an abortion—if and when *Roe v. Wade* was overturned. Only with the reaffirmation of *Roe,* and the election of Bill Clinton, did the Catholics come around. Then, at the eleventh hour, a group of state attorneys general objected to the bill on the grounds that it would provide inmates with grounds for compelling prison officials to accede to their religious demands. But the roller-coaster ride finally ended with passage by both houses of Congress, and President Clinton signed the bill into law on November 16, 1993.

At the end of the year, the annual Gallup survey of important religion stories disclosed that passage of the act hadn't registered at all with the general public.[20] According to the Associated Press on December 29, religion newswriters ranked it seventh on their list of the year's ten most important religion stories, behind the World Parliament of Religions meeting in Chicago and the bombing of the World

Trade Center and ahead of the release of the study draft of a Lutheran report on human sexuality.

During a session with reporters in the White House in December, Clinton criticized the secular media for their lack of attention to RFRA. The law, he said, "affected the lives of people in a profound way."[21] Clinton, an enthusiast of Stephen Carter's book, may well have believed this to represent another case of the "culture of disbelief." Yet it is important to note that the campaign for passage was a campaign largely of religious and civil liberties lobbying groups and their lawyers, not pastors and people in the pews. By comparison, President Harry Truman's abortive effort to appoint an ambassador to the Vatican involved mass demonstrations and a large volume of mail to Congress. After it was all over, James M. Dunn, executive director of the Baptist Joint Committee (which coordinated the RFRA campaign), criticized "the denominational headquarters, the churches out over the country, the pulpits of America, the church-related colleges and seminaries" for doing "pitifully little" to promote the bill. "Too often as the Washington hired hands of all these groups went out over the nation, it seemed that no one knew or cared about RFRA."[22]

Why was this? In the midst of the campaign, Michael Farris, president of the Home School Legal Defense Association, told a reporter that he had "dedicated his life" to trying to teach the evangelical community that free-exercise issues were far more important than establishment-clause ones. "Their ability to worship is far more important than someone giving a twenty-second prayer at a high school graduation," he said.[23] But to evangelicals, as to many other religious Americans, the dangers seemed remote and theoretical. As Nancy Ammerman, a sociologist of religion, pointed out when speaking of her co-religionists, "The vast majority of Southern Baptists aren't engaged in anything they can imagine the government wanting to interfere with."[24] And, it could be added, there is some suspicion of those who are so engaged.

More might nonetheless have been expected from the news media, which, in the face of outright public opposition, will take up cudgels on behalf of the free-speech rights of political extremists and the desires of avant-garde artists to obtain federal grants. But the religious practices that seek protection under the free exercise clause are frequently eccentric in ways that offend the sensibilities of the media as much as they offend the public at large.

NOTES

1. It is not, to be sure, the only message conveyed by the Christian tradition. Five chapters after the passage quoted, Jesus informs his disciples: "Think not that I am come to send peace on earth; I came not to send peace, but a sword" (Matt. 10:34). As Gedaliahu Stroumsa, a historian of comparative religion, points out, there have been two diametrically opposed approaches to resolving the ambiguity of Christianity in this regard: Edward Gibbon's view that an intrinsically intolerant Christianity corrupted the tolerant Roman state after it was adopted as the state religion in the fourth century, and the Christian apologetic view that it was the Roman state that corrupted a fundamentally tolerant Christianity. Neither view, Stroumsa argues, does justice to the complexity of the historical situation. Stroumsa, "Le radicalisme religieux du premier Christianisme: Contexte et implications," in *Les retours aux écritures: Fondamentalismes présents et passés,* ed. Évelyne Patlagean and Alain LeBoulluec (Louvain-Paris: Peeters, 1994), 373.

2. Gordon W. Allport and J. Michael Ross, "Personal Religious Orientation and Prejudice," *Journal of Personality and Social Psychology* 5, no. 4 (1967): 432–43.

3. In the following discussion I am indebted to Donald Frederick Brod's study, "Church, State, and Press: Twentieth-Century Episodes in the United States," unpublished Ph.D. diss., University of Minnesota, 1968, ch. 5. Of the newspapers Brod examined, the *Herald Tribune* was the most vehemently anti-Smith.

4. Brod, "Church, State, and Press," 282.

5. The same cannot be said for the *Los Angeles Times,* which on October 25 published an editorial cartoon captioned "Mad Bomber," in which a donkey, labeled "Kennedy camp followers," was depicted tossing a bomb labeled "Religious Issue Exploitation."

6. Brod, "Church, State, and Press," 359.

7. Ibid., 245. The *Tribune* was a "wet" newspaper editorially.

8. Garry Wills and Stephen L. Carter, in books on religion in American politics and culture, level the different but related charge that the media ignore or paper over the religious commitments of those politicians they approve of but highlight the faith of those they dislike. See Wills, *Under God: Religion and American Politics* (New York: Simon and Schuster, 1990), 63; and Carter, *The Culture of Disbelief: How American Law and Politics Trivialize Religious Devotion* (New York: Basic Books, 1993), 59–60.

9. There was more than a twinge of hypocrisy in this statement, inasmuch as Christian conservatives (including black ones) had vigorously criticized the civil rights activism of Martin Luther King, Jr., and the National Council of Churches had for decades been denounced by the organs of evangelicalism.

10. In Dallas on August 22, 1980, Ronald Reagan disingenuously told the National Affairs Briefing of the Religious Roundtable, "I know you cannot endorse me, but I endorse you and everything you do." The briefing, designed by Republican party operatives and conservative evangelical leaders, effectively marked the creation of the Christian Right as a wing of the G.O.P.

11. *New York Times,* November 9, 1980.

12. *Newsweek,* September 17, 1984, 24–35.

13. *Christian Century,* March 2, 1988, 203.

14. *Washington Post,* December 5, 1989.

15. *Atlanta Journal,* June 9, 1992. The charge that the liberals were the truly intolerant ones had long since become a staple of the rhetoric of the religious right — proof positive of the force of the tolerance topos in American society at large. See James Davison Hunter, *Culture Wars: The Struggle to Define America* (New York: Basic Books, 1991), 149.

16. See Glen Jeansonne, "Religious Bigotry and the Press: The Treatment of Gerald L. K. Smith," in *Reporting Religion: Facts and Faith,* ed. Benjamin J. Hubbard (Sonoma: Polebridge Press, 1990), 177–91; an earlier article by Jeansonne covering the same territory is "Combating Anti-Semitism: The Case of Gerald L. K. Smith," in *Anti-Semitism in American History,* ed. David A. Gerber (Urbana: University of Illinois Press, 1986), 152–66.

17. Leonard Levy, "School Prayers and the Founding Fathers," *Commentary* 34 (September 1962): 230. For an analysis of press coverage of the 1962 prayer decision, see William A. Hachten, "Journalism and the Prayer Decision," *Columbia Journalism Review* 2 (Fall 1962): 4–9.

18. For example: "Better for all to learn religious tolerance than beam their particular prayers to a society of diverse faiths" (*New York Times,* December 8, 1993), or, "The ban on public school prayer is described as both proof and cause of what many see as this country's moral decline, and of its lack of respect for religion. The exact opposite is true. The ban on public school prayer reflects instead a deeply profound respect for religion and its place in human lives. It recognizes the fundamental importance of keeping government as far as possible from infringing on an individual's right of free conscience" (*Atlanta Constitution,* December 25, 1993).

19. *Time,* December 20, 1993, 41; *Atlanta Journal-Constitution,* December 14, 1993.

20. Religious News Service, December 29, 1993.

21. Religious News Service, December 17, 1993.

22. James M. Dunn, "Reflections," *Report from the Capital* (November-December, 1993): 15. Dunn also took the press to task for ignoring RFRA.

23. Telephone interview with the author, January 1993.

24. Telephone interview with the author, November 1993.

CHAPTER SEVEN

Hypocrisy

Woe unto you, scribes and Pharisees, hypocrites!
for ye are like unto whited sepulchres, which indeed appear beautiful outward, but are within full
of dead men's bones, and of all uncleanness.

MATTHEW 23:27

When Sinclair Lewis's novel *Elmer Gantry* appeared in 1927, mass revivalism was on the ropes in American culture. Concerned about irresponsible and unscrupulous evangelistic behavior, the Federal Council of Churches had fifteen years earlier established a Commission
on Evangelism to monitor some two thousand evangelists nationwide. In 1917, John D. Rockefeller, Jr., conducted an investigation of
the financial practices of the prince of contemporary revivalists, Billy
Sunday.[1] And in 1926, the country wallowed in the story of the myste-
rious three-day disappearance of the Pentecostal queen Aimee Semple
McPherson—alleged by her to have been a kidnapping, alleged by
her enemies to have been a secret tryst with a married former em-
ployee. In the heyday of Progressivism, revivalists had made a spe-
ciality of campaigning against bars, bawdyhouses, and the personal
immorality that led folks to them. Accounts of their own moral lapses
were therefore particularly shocking to some, particularly delicious to
others. Helped by the longstanding distrust of revivalism in ecclesiastical circles, the image of the corrupt evangelist became paradigmatic
of religious hypocrisy in American culture.

It is worth recalling, however, that Lewis's smoking, boozing,
philandering, acquisitive preacher was not just a revivalist. Midway
through the novel, Gantry's career with the Aimee-like Sharon Fal-

coner comes to its fiery end, and he begins working his way up the hierarchy of the Methodist church—aided and abetted by the news media.

There was, perhaps, no preacher in Zenith, not even the liberal Unitarian minister or the powerful Catholic bishop, who was not fond of the young gentlemen of the press. The newspapers of Zenith were as likely to attack religion as they were to attack the department-stores. But of all the clerics, none was so hearty, so friendly, so brotherly, to the reporters as the Reverend Elmer Gantry. His rival parsons were merely cordial to the sources of publicity when they called. Elmer did his own calling.

Gantry enlists the newspapers in his campaign to root out vice in the city. Zenith's leading publisher orders his sermons reported at least once a month. Taking advantage of the new technology, Gantry becomes the first clergyman in the state to have his services broadcast by radio. In the novel's climax, he is almost brought low when his affair with the church secretary is uncovered by the sole reporter who sees through him. The reporter writes a story about the secretary's husband's threatened lawsuit for alienation of affection and the entire press has a field day with the scandal. But after the woman is prevailed upon to recant, the newspapers "joyfully" announce Gantry's innocence. The tale ends with the redeemed preacher promising his cheering congregation, "We shall yet make these United States a moral nation."[2]

For the mass media, however, this portrait of the compleat religious hypocrite was too strong by half. When Hollywood took up the story in 1960, it jettisoned Gantry's career as a church minister as well as the novel's morally uncomfortable ending. All that was seen was the hypocrite-revivalist, with revivalism presented as the source of the problem. Lest anyone think that the problem was religion itself, an opening disclaimer declared:

We believe that certain aspects of revivalism can bear examination—that the conduct of some revivalists makes a mockery of the traditional beliefs and practices of Christianity!

We believe that everyone has a right to worship according to his conscience, but Freedom of Religion is not license to abuse the faith of the people!

However, due to the highly controversial nature of this film, we strongly urge you to prevent impressionable children from seeing it!

It would have been more accurate to say that Freedom of Religion is precisely license to abuse the faith of the people (whatever that is), but that Freedom of Speech is license to criticize such religious practices as may be deemed abusive. In any event, the role of protector of the people's faith is assigned to the gimlet-eyed newspaper reporter. "What is a revival?" he asks, rhetorically. "Is it a church? Is it a religion? Or is it a circus sideshow, complete with freaks, magic, and rabble rousing?" Of Gantry himself he demands, "What gives you the right to speak God's word?"

But if Hollywood hateth the sin, it loveth the sinner. The movie takes the edge off Lewis's dark fable by permitting Burt Lancaster's Gantry to repent of his evil ways. In the final scene, as Sharon Falconer's tabernacle-on-the-pier goes up in flames, he heroically helps rescue survivors from the water (instead of merely pretending to rescue them, as in the novel); and when asked to pick up where the now deceased lady evangelist has left off, he quotes St. Paul: "I put away childish things." A similar redemption is accomplished in *Leap of Faith*, a much lighter-hearted 1992 film about a charlatan faith healer. There, it is after a bona fide healing takes place that the Rev. Jonas Nightingale (Steve Martin) is able to put aside his private war with religion and leave the traveling tent show to those of greater faith.

Curiously enough, the movie version of the Gantry story appeared in the wake of Billy Graham's remarkable resuscitation of urban mass revivalism in America. Graham, despite some theological carping and an unfortunate political entanglement with Richard Nixon, not only made revivalism respectable again but also made himself into the country's most prominent and respected Protestant leader. On the occasion of his seventy-fifth birthday in 1993, *Time* put him on the cover as "A Christian in Winter," retelling the familiar stories of how he had once upon a time been promoted by the aged William Randolph Hearst and how he had dealt with the endemic temptations of his trade by forswearing free-will offerings in favor of fixed salaries and adopting a policy never to be alone with a woman other than his wife. If a greater big-time evangelist ever comes along, the magazine declared, "That will truly be a miracle."[3]

In the meantime, however, the scandals that had once bedeviled revivalism had returned with a vengeance. Jim and Tammy Faye Bakker
and Jimmy Swaggart, the Christian television celebrities whose ministries collapsed in scandal in 1987, were in one sense the heirs of the
old-time evangelists. They were entrepreneurial shepherds of far-flung
flocks, cable itinerants who turned living rooms into tabernacles; and
the contributions that flowed into their coffers were the old free-will
offerings writ large—very large. Yet they were also after the manner of
settled clergy: Swaggart with his huge campus in Baton Rouge, Louisiana, and the Bakkers with Heritage, U.S.A., the theme park of the
PTL (Praise The Lord, People That Love) ministry that in its heyday
drew more visitors than all theme parks save Disney's. The Bakkers
were Pentecostals gone upscale and sentimental; their Holy Spirit announced a gospel of material prosperity. This disgusted Swaggart, the
fellow Pentecostal who preached the old-time religion of brimstone
and sins washed clean in the blood of the Lamb. When their shaky PTL
empire collapsed amid charges that Bakker had forced himself sexually on a supposedly virginal church secretary, Swaggart delighted in
the fall from grace. But hardly had the Bakkers fallen than he himself
was revealed to have frequented a prostitute in a seedy motel outside
New Orleans.

The news media went crazy over the two scandals, from the tabloids to the *New York Times,* from shock radio to "Nightline." *Penthouse* published no fewer than seven articles on one or another' aspect of the story, including, in July 1988, a notorious, black-and-white
photo spread of the very prostitute whom Swaggart visited, in the self-
same motel room, demonstrating the self-same poses. Here was Swaggart denouncing the enslavement of pornography, cheek by jowl with
Swaggart asking that she do "like a magazine I've seen." It was, said the
magazine, "the scandal of the century." In fact, the Bakker-Swaggart
affair bore some resemblance to the Aimee Semple McPherson story.
Like her, the principals were Pentecostal celebrities, famous nationwide but hardly from the mainstream of American religious life. Just
as her main opponents were other California clergy, so was their fracas
dubbed a "Holy War," not only because of Swaggart's verbal assaults
but also for the struggle that ensued when the Baptist Jerry Falwell,
brought in to keep PTL afloat, shrank back in horror after looking
at the books. The most instructive comparison, however, is with the
"scandal of the century" before, the grandaddy of all religious media

events, the 1874–75 adultery case against the Rev. Henry Ward Beecher of Plymouth Congregationalist Church in Brooklyn, New York.

Beecher was the silver-tongued embodiment of Protestant liberalism, a man whose good cheer, sentimental piety, and support for social uplift — dispersed on the lecture circuit and in an unending stream of religious journalism — made him the most prominent and sought-after minister in the country. His church was huge and built along the lines of a theatrical auditorium; his salary was huge as well. He stood accused of having had an affair with the wife of a close friend and sometime journalistic associate, a parishioner with whom he had fallen out. The tale was wrapped up in the women's rights movement, which Beecher staunchly supported, and featured a series of accusations and recantations by the supposed inamorata, payoffs to the husband, and a six-month-long trial in Brooklyn City Court.

Some, like Charles A. Dana of the *New York Sun,* had long considered Beecher a hypocrite and saw the alleged affair as a vindication of their views. In 1875, the *Sun* devoted nearly two hundred editorials to the case and more than 120 tightly packed columns. The rest of the New York press followed closely behind, and coverage blanketed the rest of the country, too. To Beecher's many supporters (who far outnumbered his detractors), it was as if the fate of American Protestantism hung in the balance. Consider the following dispatch from Brooklyn published in the *Charleston* [S.C.] *News and Courier* amid the presentation of evidence to a church committee that Beecher specially convened in the summer of 1874 to conduct an examination.

The week closed yesterday on the most agonizing six consecutive days in social history. My pen would utterly fail to give adequate description of the excitement that prevailed. Imagine, though, a whole city talking day and night upon one subject, and scarcely talking of anything else; imagine the daily papers teeming with editorials, interviews, and fresh statements, all headed with large startling headlines. . . . The corrupting influence of the scandal upon public morals can scarcely be over-estimated. Here is a subject that under ordinary circumstances would be tabooed in decent society. But because a great clergyman is involved it necessarily fills the thoughts of everybody. The turning over of the vile details in the mind day and night for a week, and their open discussion from every point of view, have had the effect of breaking down barriers which modesty has erected, and leaving the community a great deal worse off than when the trouble began. There is but one chance of a recovery from this miserable state of things, and that is the successful vindication of Henry Ward Beecher. . . . No greater blow could be struck at the morality of the generation than the fall of its most powerful advocate.[4]

In fact, Beecher *was* vindicated, more or less. The church committee exonerated him of all charges, while the jury in the civil suit failed to reach a verdict, splitting nine to three in favor of acquittal. Whether Beecher actually committed adultery is still a matter of historical disagreement, but for the great mass of his supporters, it seemed inconceivable that he could be guilty. After the trial, Plymouth Church raised $100,000 for his legal expenses, and admirers mobbed him when he went out lecturing. With no apparent loss of prestige, he resumed his place at the helm of Protestant America.[5]

It is not hard to understand why the nineteenth-century press should have been consumed with the fate of Henry Ward Beecher. But why should the news media of the 1980s have made such fuss about Jimmy Swaggart and the Bakkers? In contrast to the Beecher affair, where the press was largely an onlooker at judicial proceedings, the news media actually played a crucial investigative role in exposing the financial shenanigans at PTL as well as the various sexual misdeeds — adulterous, homosexual, sodomistic, and otherwise.

Coverage in the most responsible news organizations was less than clear about why the story seemed so big. The *Charlotte Observer,* PTL's hometown newspaper, led the investigative way, focusing on the Bakkers' use of viewers' contributions to support their own lavish life-style rather than pious good works. The newspaper focused as well on the sale of time-sharing deals in nonexistent Heritage hotels, the fraud that ultimately got Jim Bakker and several associates convicted in federal court. "I was covering this as a corrupt business," said Charles Shepard, the *Observer* reporter who won a Pulitzer Prize for his efforts.[6] Yet while PTL was a multi-million-dollar operation, there have been many other lucrative business scams that never received a fraction of the ink.

By contrast, the sexual aspects of the story, which the *Washington Post*'s intrepid Art Harris exposed with great verve, seemed to sink farther and farther into tabloidism. Did Tammy Faye Bakker's crush

on a "flashy country singer" push her husband into the arms of church
secretary Jessica Hahn? Was Hahn the deflowered virgin she made
herself out to be or, as Bakker claimed, a sexual manipulator who
knew all the tricks of the trade? "Some of the questions, which focus
on Hahn's alleged sexual experience, seem curiously Victorian," Harris acknowledged, concluding somewhat lamely that they were legitimate because Hahn had asserted her victimhood herself and ridden it
to national celebrity.[7] But why should anyone care?

It took the more freewheeling media to make the real issues explicit. Freelancing for *Penthouse,* Harris and *Post* colleague Michael
Isikoff called the PTL story a "saga of sex, sin and pseudosalvation, a
litany of excess and hypocrisy from the pulpit."[8] As for Jimmy Swaggart, Harris and Jason Berry wrote, "[E]ven as he was railing against
the immorality of others, playing Pentecostal inquisitor to rival televangelists . . . [he] was furtively cruising for sex, wrestling Satan and
his own dark urges down on the bayou."[9] Later, following up the story
as a reporter for CNN on June 8, 1991, Harris asked Marvin Gorman,
the fellow evangelist who caught Swaggart leaving the motel, whether
he thought Swaggart cared "more about morality or market share."
Gorman, Harris reported, had demanded of Swaggart how he could
"be such a hypocrite."

In an interview, Harris readily agreed that hypocrisy was the bottom line in the whole Bakker-Swaggart affair: "It was a perversion
of religion pure and simple." Similarly, in his book on PTL, Charles
Shepard allowed as how, for most Americans, the story was really
about "the latest hypocrite to sully the revival tent with greed and
adultery"—and gave himself leeway to speak of Bakker's "wholesale
failure as a moral leader."[10] Hypocrisy, it need hardly be added, is not
a violation of law. It is a deeply embedded Western religious concept,
taken from a Greek term for play-acting and used in Job, Isaiah, and
the Gospels to denote the false pretense of piety and virtue.

Of course, it is difficult to imagine American males with their
Penthouses being scandalized by the Bakker-Swaggart hypocrisies
the way the *News and Courier's* correspondent was scandalized by
l'affaire Beecher in 1874. Was most of the public interest just prurient?
Ted Koppel of "Nightline," confessing his fascination with the story,
pointed his finger at the mirror: "It has revealed the hypocrisy that
is buried just beneath the surface in most of us—claiming to be in-
censed, even outraged, by what we hear, all the while clamoring for

more."[11] Whether public anger was real or feigned is beside the point. The topos of religious hypocrisy is irresistible for public and media alike, particularly when the hypocrites are as weepy and sanctimonious as Swaggart and the Bakkers. Living by the media, they deserved to perish by the media.

The scandals also came along at the right cultural moment. Like the early part of the century, the 1980s were a time when evangelical Protestants were on the march. Although neither Swaggart nor the Bakkers engaged heavily in politics, many were prepared to include them among the evangelical crusaders who deserved a comeuppance for demanding that others toe the line of their professed morality. But for all that, the news coverage of the scandals drew little criticism from the forces of evangelicalism.

Jerry Falwell, hardly a favorite of the liberal media, came out of the story well. *Newsweek* sprinkled its account of the last days of PTL with italicized quotes from Falwell expressing shocked outrage at what the Bakkers had wrought. "Falwell," wrote Charles Shepard, "brought to PTL a set of absolute standards—a crucible that Bakker could not survive."[12] Nor did Falwell shrink from returning the compliment. In an address to AP editors, he praised the *Charlotte Observer* and "other periodicals" for "forcing us" to make financial disclosure. Coverage of the Bakker scandal had in fact been "good for Christianity," he said. "All of us Christian leaders . . . have been pretty independent and fairly arrogant, hiding behind the First Amendment. We've been saying it's no one's business how much money we take in and where it goes. It is the public's business."[13] Out in the evangelical hinterland, the reaction seemed to be the same. As Dan Morgan noted in *Rising in the West,* his book about a fundamentalist Okie family in California, "To those outside the fold, the adultery of Jim Bakker, the peccadilloes of [Jimmy] Swaggart, the financial difficulties of [Oral] Roberts, and [Pat] Robertson's political self-destruction seemed bizarre and outlandish. But for those within the fold, it was part of a natural cycle in which God cut down to size those who had lost track of their place and their mission."[14]

After his conviction for fraud and conspiracy, Jim Bakker was sentenced by U.S. District Judge Robert D. Potter to forty-five years in prison—a term vastly out of line with federal sentencing guidelines. Bakker, said Potter, "had no thought whatever about his victims, and those of us who do have a religion are ridiculed as being saps [for] money-grubbing preachers and priests." Citing the remark, an appeals court later overturned the sentence.[15] Yet the judge had imprudently disclosed the larger cultural truth. What had happened at PTL, what Jimmy Swaggart had done, was not just a private matter, was not just financial fraud and sexual peccadillo. It was an abuse of the faith of their followers and, by extension, of all believers. At bottom, that is what the topos of religious hypocrisy is all about, and why there was a remarkably united front of media, evangelicals, *Penthouse* readers, and "Nightline" watchers to heap abuse upon the hypocrites.

By way of contrast, a word needs to be said about the coverage of Catholic priests charged with sexually abusing children and adolescents. These too were stories of hypocrisy, of whited sepulchers filled with uncleanness. Yet the Bakker-Swaggart saga was high comedy compared with the grim accounts of people psychologically maimed for life by religious leaders who had been entrusted with their care. Where the Assemblies of God had no trouble expelling Bakker and Swaggart, the Catholic church waffled — first reacting defensively, then admitting the problem, then turning again to hardball legal tactics.[16] The story also got tangled up in larger questions concerning the shortage of priests and the merits of clerical celibacy. That celibacy was the problem became a topos of its own — one that the prolific Andrew Greeley felt called upon to condemn in the pages of *Newsweek* as anti-Catholic bigotry.[17] Priest abuse was, in short, not a simple and satisfying morality tale, but a complex and deeply troubling set of narratives about sex offenders and institutional failure. Not surprisingly, the news media were reluctant to become involved until the going got safe.

Jason Berry, the Louisiana freelancer who almost single-handedly exposed the extent of child abuse in the church, has described his futile efforts to interest leading national publications in the story.[18] Charles Sennott found a similar reaction when, as a reporter for the *New York Post*, he began to pursue allegations of sexual abuse against Bruce Ritter, the Franciscan priest who ran a huge mission for runaway adolescents called Covenant House. The topos that attached to Ritter was good works, and fellow journalists were not interested in hearing about anything else. As Sennott put it, "The man was legendary among those who knew his tireless work on behalf of troubled young people nationwide."[19] All this should be borne in mind when considering Cardinal Law's attack on the *Boston Globe* for aggressively pursuing a pedophile story (chapter 1), or the charges of overzealous media that accompanied reports of abuse charges filed (and later withdrawn) against Cardinal Joseph Bernardin of Chicago.[20]

The followers of Bakker and Swaggart may have been disillusioned by their religious heroes and discouraged from contributing again to television ministries, but if any of them were shaken in their beliefs, no one bothered to report it. That was not the case with stories about priestly sexual misconduct. "I lost my faith," said a woman on camera in a March 21, 1993 "60 Minutes" segment on the affairs of Archbishop Robert Sanchez of Albuquerque. She could almost have been speaking for Berry and Sennott, Catholics both, who made clear that their reporting cost them spiritually. "Frankly, I didn't believe the allegations—or at least I didn't want to believe them," wrote Sennott. "My Irish Catholic roots were showing, and years of learned deference to men of the cloth were hard to overcome."[21] Wrote Berry: "Finally, this is a book about faith—my own, and that of others drawn into a maelstrom much larger than ourselves. The journey of this troubled believer was slowly engulfed by the agonizing quest for justice of people from as far afield as Newfoundland and Hawaii. Pulled along by currents of their lives, I witnessed courage and grace in ways that humble me still."[22] Pursuing hypocrites can be fun and games, but it can also be the dark night of the soul.

NOTES

1. William G. McLoughlin, Jr., *Modern Revivalism: From Charles Grandison Finney to Billy Graham* (New York: Ronald Press, 1959), 447–49.

2. Sinclair Lewis, *Elmer Gantry* (New York: Harcourt Brace, 1927; New York: NAL Penguin, 1980), 414, 416.

3. *Time*, November 15, 1993, 78.

4. *News and Courier*, July 30, 1874, quoted in Kenneth Dayton Nordin, "Consensus Religion: National Newspaper Coverage of Religious Life in America, 1849–1960," unpublished Ph.D. diss., University of Michigan, 1975, 95.

5. For a good account of the case and the public response to it, see Clifford E. Clark, Jr., *Henry Ward Beecher: Spokesman for a Middle-Class America* (Urbana: University of Illinois Press, 1978), 197–232.

6. Telephone interview with the author, March 1994.

7. *Washington Post*, April 2, 1987, and September 30, 1987.

8. Art Harris and Michael Isikoff, "Empire of Excess," *Penthouse* (April 1988): 42.

9. Art Harris and Jason Berry, "Jimmy Swaggart's Secret Sex Life," *Penthouse* (July 1988): 104.

10. Charles E. Shepard, *Forgiven: The Rise and Fall of Jim Bakker and the PTL Ministry* (New York: Atlantic Monthly Press, 1989), xiii, 560.

11. Quoted in *Newsweek,* June 8, 1987, 58.

12. Shepard, *Forgiven,* 560.

13. *Editor and Publisher,* October 10, 1987, 17.

14. Dan Morgan, *Rising in the West* (New York: Alfred A. Knopf, 1992), 483.

15. *Atlanta Journal,* February 12, 1991.

16. See, for example, two articles by Jason Berry in the *Atlanta Journal-Constitution:* "Catholics Are Lifting the Lid on Abuse" (June 13, 1993), and "Church Strikes Back at Priests' Accusers" (May 1, 1994).

17. Andrew Greeley, "A View from the Priesthood," *Newsweek,* August 16, 1993, 45.

18. Jason Berry, *Lead Us Not into Temptation* (New York: Doubleday, 1992), 32.

19. Charles M. Sennott, *Broken Covenant* (New York: Simon and Schuster, 1992), 14.

20. For example, see "Cardinal Bernardin: Guilty until Proven Innocent," *Catholic League Newsletter* (December 1993), 1, 6.

21. Sennott, *Broken Covenant,* 14.

22. Berry, *Lead Us Not into Temptation,* xxi.

CHAPTER EIGHT

False Prophecy

Beware of false prophets, which come to you in
sheep's clothing, but inwardly they are ravening
wolves. Ye shall know them by their fruits.
MATTHEW 7:15–16

Hypocrisy takes place within the fold. Whether associated with practices like revivalism or televangelism, or doctrines like the prosperity
gospel, it is fundamentally a topos of personal moral defect that
charges religious leaders with violating norms of behavior that they
(are presumed to) profess. When those norms are rejected as a matter
of religious doctrine, then the religion itself can be called into question by way of the topos of false prophecy. A false prophet may be
portrayed as sincere or hypocritical, but either way, he (or she) is an
affront to the social order.

If the oldest American religious prejudice is anti-Catholicism, the
paradigm of false prophecy in the American media can be found in
coverage of the Mormon church in the nineteenth century. In the
early 1840s, while the Latter-day Saints were still in Nauvoo, Illinois, their public image was established through hostile newspaper
accounts in the *Warsaw* [Ill.] *Signal* and widely published exposés by
an excommunicated disciple named John C. Bennett.[1] Once the Mormons relocated to Salt Lake, the rest of the world was, as Jan Shipps
has pointed out, almost entirely dependent on journalistic reports for
its picture of the faith.[2] Recognizing this, Mormons themselves would
eventually pay calls on the nation's leading newspapers in an effort to
blunt anti-Mormon campaigns led by evangelical Protestant clergy.[3]

Although many of the journalists who trooped out to Salt Lake to interview Brigham Young came away impressed with the man and his people, they had little use for the religion. Calling Mormonism "a delusion and a blight," Horace Greeley of the *New York Tribune* expressed the hope that its adherents might live "to unlearn their errors, and enjoy the rich fruits of their industry, frugality, and sincere, though misguided piety!"[4] The heart of Mormon darkness was the institution of plural marriage, which before the Civil War the new Republican party paired with slavery as the nation's "twin relics of barbarism." Polygamy, Greeley declared to Brigham Young himself, was "the grave question on which your doctrines and practices are avowedly at war with those of the Christian world."[5]

In fact, the nineteenth-century press was not always prepared to join crusades against unconventional marital arrangements. In the 1870s, when local Protestants went on the warpath against the Oneida community of John Humphrey Noyes, both local and out-of-town newspapers showed themselves skeptical. As contrary to Victorian family values as Noyes's doctrine of "complex marriage" was, his well-regulated community had been around for decades. "A foul and corrupt fountain cannot send forth a stream so clear and thrifty, respectable and peaceful," noted the *Fulton Times*. Not false prophecy but clerical hypocrisy was the apposite topos for the satirical weekly *Puck,* which accused the anti-Noyes crusaders of secretly practicing what Oneida openly preached: "And this is the bare and simple statement why the gentleman in the white choker regards the Oneida Community as a Blot and Blotch and Festering Sore and an Ulcer and a Canker and all sorts of things upon the civilization of America."[6]

But Oneida was small and self-contained. The Mormon kingdom in the heart of the western wilderness was pregnant with meaning for the country as a whole, especially as the issue of Utah's statehood came to the fore. Like Roman Catholicism only more so, the LDS church was charged with exercising "un-American" social control over its adherents, and with wielding huge economic power to the detriment of their Gentile neighbors. Surely a theocratic polity based on the degradation of women could not be granted full legitimacy in the United States!

In the political lexicon of a later day, the evil of polygamy served as the "wedge issue" for anti-Mormonism. It was also the dominant topos of media coverage, according to Jan Shipps's content analysis of the treatment of Mormons in American periodicals. Before Utah was accepted for statehood in 1895 — five years after the LDS church, under intense federal pressure, officially abandoned the doctrine of plural marriage—two-thirds of all articles about Mormonism laid major or great stress on polygamy, whereas but half dealt with (for example) political matters. Fully 85 percent of all the articles were negative; more than 60 percent, "extremely negative." The articles did not, for the most part, treat Mormon plural marriage in terms of sexual licentiousness (although that concept presumably occurred to the Victorian reader's imagination). Rather, the topos highmindedly had to do with the threat that religiously sanctioned polygamy posed to the norms of conjugal life—and, for advanced thinkers like Greeley, to prospects for enhancing women's rights and opportunities in American society.[7] In Shipps's words, "Political power could be dealt with. A society in which men had more than one wife could not." Indeed, for several decades after 1895, polygamy remained the principal fruit by which Mormonism was known—the most prominent element of articles that were nearly as hostile toward the religion as those of the earlier period.[8]

This longstanding preoccupation with the evil of polygamy expressed an aversion to the exploitation of women that has been an element of the false-prophecy topos since the first days of the penny press. In 1834–35, papers in New York and around the country became fascinated with the story of Robert Matthews, a flamboyant religious figure who attracted a tiny flock of middle-class followers under his patriarchal leadership as the "Hebrew prophet Matthias." In their fine retelling of the story, Paul Johnson and Sean Wilentz show how Matthias was motivated by hatred of the increasingly feminist evangelical Protestant mainstream and point out that such "longings for a supposedly bygone holy patriarchy" have characterized American prophetic groups down to the present day.[9]

In its 1879 *Reynolds* decision denying First Amendment protection for Mormon polygamy, the U.S. Supreme Court famously declared, "Laws are made for the government of actions and while they cannot interfere with mere religious beliefs and opinions, they may with practices."[10] Through the subsequent ebb and flow of free-exercise jurisprudence, the constitutional challenge has been to define a standard under which such interference is warranted. Before *Smith v. Employment Division,* and again under the Religious Freedom Restoration Act, the standard has been "strict scrutiny": Before a religious practice can be barred, a "compelling state interest" must be demonstrated.

Yet *Reynolds, Smith,* and many "strict scrutiny" decisions themselves
point to a long-standing judicial readiness to suppress religious practices that do little more than violate social rules and conventions.
In society at large, unconventional conduct can actually seem more
dangerous, more in need of suppression, when performed under the
legitimating auspices of religion. At the same time, when new and
eccentric religious groups come upon the scene, there tends to be a
search for objectionable behavior, whether or not it exists. For it is by
the fruit of immoral and illegal acts that such groups can be known —
and dragged out from under the First Amendment's protection.

In a study of American, German, and Dutch print-media coverage
of the downfall of the Rajneeshee commune in Antelope, Oregon, in
1985, Barry van Driel and Jacob van Belzen found that the American
media laid by far the most emphasis on the criminal aspects of the
story.[11] There was, to be sure, criminal activity to write about concerning the Bhagwan Shree Rajneesh and, especially, his chief executive
and intermediary Ma Anand Sheela. Yet the press in Germany and
the Netherlands, where the bhagwan had a significant number of followers, took a more nuanced view of the situation. Newspapers in the
Netherlands made Sheela the focus of negative coverage, balancing accounts of the bhagwan and the Rajneeshee movement as a whole with
positive appreciation. Although the German press was more negative, its focus was on the movement "as a deviant group with bizarre
beliefs and rituals." The American press treated it as a criminal enterprise that had to be exposed. Thus the Portland *Oregonian,* which
conducted the most thorough investigation of the Rajneeshees, spent
a large amount of time fruitlessly trying to track down a report that
the movement was engaged in the drug trade. This criminal focus not
only denied the movement religious legitimacy, but also rendered its
spiritual appeal incomprehensible. As the *Oregonian's* assistant managing editor later said, "One of the things that constantly amazed me
was the majority [of ex-Rajneeshees] maintained an intense loyalty to
the bhagwan or to the movement itself."[12] To the American press, the
bhagwan was simply a false prophet preying on the gullible.[13]

This portrait of Rajneeshee press coverage dovetails with the more
comprehensive content analysis van Driel and James Richardson conducted of the American print media's treatment of new religious
movements from the early 1970s through the early 1980s. In looking at press accounts of such groups as the Unification church, the

Church of Scientology, Hare Krishna, and the Children of God, the study found that trials and criminal investigations far outranked all other subject matter. Indeed, two-and-a-half times as much attention was devoted to legal conflicts as to the actual beliefs of the groups. By comparison, articles dealing with a "control" group of more familiar marginal religious bodies (Christian Science, Jehovah's Witnesses, the Salvation Army, Mennonites/Amish) dealt twice as often with beliefs as with legal matters. Even more tellingly, the issues of brainwashing, manipulation, and psychological abuse, which occurred next in frequency to legal issues in articles about new religious movements, arose in not a single article concerning the comparison groups.[14]

This "brainwashing" sub-topos, which became the most characteristic feature of the coverage of "cults" in the early 1970s, has been interpreted by some as an expression of secular bias on the media's part. The idea of making a radical religious break with one's previous life (commonly taken as evidence of brainwashing) is a familiar feature of all conversion religions; in the Christian tradition it begins with Jesus' disciples leaving home and family for the sake of the kingdom of God (Luke 18:28–30). Presumably it is those ignorant of the character of religious conversion, or hostile to intense religious commitment, who are likely to see such adherence in terms of medical pathology. As Thomas Robbins and Dick Anthony remark:

> Behind the medicalization of cults is the latent premise that certain kinds of religion—emotionally fervent religion, stridently supernaturalist religion, authoritarian sectarianism, life-consuming religion, spiritual ecstasy and mysticism—are socially regressive and thus hostile to mankind's deepest aspirations. The cults are at least as different from each other as they are from the mainstream, but they all repudiate the modern ideal of the rationalized self.

Yet, as Robbins and Anthony also recognize, the medicalization of deviant religious groups has served the interests of religious anticultists, allowing them to "disavow intentions of persecuting beliefs" even as they demonize the alleged brainwashers.[15]

In fact, brainwashing has from the beginning had religious connotations. The concept was invented in the 1950s to explain why American prisoners of war in Korea had been so easily swayed to the views of their communist captors.[16] Not that they had, but that's another story. The point is that communism was widely regarded at the time as a species of religion, and brainwashing served to explain conversion to a false, un-American faith.[17] By an odd coincidence, the Korean connection was reestablished two decades later, when the Rev. Sun Myung Moon's messianic Unification church became a principal focus of brainwashing charges.[18] In an analysis of newspaper articles about former members of the Unification church, David Bromley, Anson Shupe, and J. C. Ventimiglia have explored the recurrence of what they call "atrocity tales" — accounts of how the church abused members in one way or another. From these tales, the former members emerge as victims of an organization that flagrantly violates what the authors describe as "fundamental cultural values." Far and away the largest number involve accounts of psychological abuse, in which the underlying theme is "the loss of individual freedom, including a personal freedom to choose a religion and the manner in which to practice it." Brainwashing thus becomes a crime against religion — than which there can be no greater justification for repression in American society. The tales serve to justify efforts to "deprogram" former church members by "construct[ing] a moral basis for otherwise illegal actions." [19]

In the final analysis, the use of the concept of brainwashing cannot be considered an expression of secular bias because it has done little to alter traditional patterns of addressing deviant religion in American culture. Just as in the nineteenth century Protestant ministers led crusades against Mormonism and the Oneida community, so, in the latter part of the twentieth, anticult activity — including deprogramming efforts — has been spearheaded by the religious. And just as the nineteenth-century press sometimes evinced skepticism at these religious crusades, so the media of the late twentieth century have been willing to entertain doubts about the activities of religiously inspired deprogrammers.[20] Overall, the effect has been merely to give a psychological cast to traditional concerns about false prophecy in America — how it fosters the (un-American) subordination of individual religious conscience to theocratic social control. That this point of view reflects a distinctively Protestant conception of religious conscience cannot be doubted.

A classic example of the false-prophecy topos may be found in *Time* magazine's May 6, 1991, cover story, "Scientology: Cult of Greed." [21] The story begins with an atrocity tale of a young Scientologist who committed suicide and quotes "psychiatrists" as saying that the church's famous auditing sessions can produce a "drugged-like, mind-controlled euphoria that keeps customers coming back for more." This portrait of adherents as brainwashed victims is the only explicit explanation offered for why anyone would be attracted to Scientology. However, there is a suggestion, in a series of tales about Scientologists who have engaged in unscrupulous business practices, that the religion has enabled them to prosper by teaching immorality. Throughout, Scientology is portrayed as a "depraved yet thriving enterprise" that has "shielded itself exquisitely behind the First Amendment." Leader L. Ron Hubbard, who once referred to potential converts as "raw meat," represents the quintessential incarnation of false prophet as ravening wolf.

Not all media accounts of marginal religious groups trade equally heavily in the false-prophet topos, even when dealing with a group like Scientology. In a massive series of articles published in 1990, the *Los Angeles Times* did not hesitate to call Scientology a religion, albeit noting its "cultish image." The series steered clear of the standard charges of brainwashing and destruction of individual conscience; there was little in the way of atrocity storytelling. While vigorously pursuing evidence of the church's misdeeds, the newspaper made clear that Scientology had bona fide spiritual attractions; various rank-and-file members were quoted testifying to the good it had done them.[22] In this case, more thorough investigation made it possible to see beyond the conventions of the topos of false prophecy. The likelihood of that happening shrinks, however, when the topos is culturally hot-wired into the religious phenomenon in question. Such was the case with coverage of the bloody confrontation in Waco, Texas, between the Branch Davidians and federal authorities that held the country's attention from February 28 until April 19, 1993.

From first to last, it was hard for the news media to avoid portraying the group's leader, David Koresh, as an antichrist, the New Testament type of the false prophet. He presented himself to his followers as Jesus come again in sin, shepherding them into the End Times at the jerry-built compound first called Mount Carmel, then Ranch Apocalypse. The *Waco Tribune-Herald*'s initial newspaper series on the group, which began running the day before the abortive raid by the Bureau of Alcohol, Tobacco and Firearms, was entitled "The Sinful Messiah." *People*'s March 15 cover story, "The Evil Messiah," began,

"For someone who claimed to believe he was Jesus, David Koresh was a twisted representation of Christian ideals." In its May 3 cover story, "Tragedy in Waco," *Time* interpolated passages from Revelation into a narrative of the entire story, concluding with Rev. 20:10: "And the devil who had deceived them was thrown into the lake of fire and sulphur, where the beast and the false prophet were, and they will be tormented day and night forever and ever." But nothing equaled *Time*'s March 15 cover, which set up, like twin caryatids of evil, distorted photos of Koresh and Sheik Omar Abdel-Rahman (spiritual leader of a suspect in the bombing of New York's World Trade Center) flanking a black space that read:

IN

THE

NAME

OF

GOD

What happens
when believers
embrace the
dark side of faith

Leaving no stone unturned, the inside coverage also dealt with the ethno-religious war in Bosnia. "Sometimes," *Time* opined, "it is the faithful of the churches, and the mosques, who need policing most of all."[23]

Unlike the sheik, who (*Time* reported) actually condemned the World Trade Center bombing, there never was any question that Koresh was the false prophet he appeared to be. What remained a conundrum for the media was deciding which violations of the moral order might justify the needed policing. Indeed, throughout the two-month saga, and during the aftermath of investigation and trial, the Branch Davidian story never acquired the clear moral focus of, say, the mass suicide of Jim Jones's followers in the Guyana jungle in 1978.

"How long before they will act?" demanded the *Tribune-Herald* in a first-day editorial that assailed local law enforcement authorities for failing to step in "when young girls are sexually exploited in the name of religion." While acknowledging that the Branch Davidians' status as a "religious body" might explain this official reluctance to move against the group, the editorial argued that "the right to religious freedom doesn't include the right to abuse others." There was, however, something disingenuous in this charge of law-enforcement inertness. After the botched raid, the newspaper's editor, Bob Lott, informed readers that ATF officials had asked the paper to hold off its series, hinting that they were about to take action. Instead, the paper decided that what was going on was a "dangerous and sinister thing," a "menace in our community," that the public needed to know about. "We're not talking just of stockpiling of weapons, but such things as sexual exploitation of young girls and other abuses of children in the name of religion." He did not make clear exactly how the wider community was menaced by all this.[24]

From the *Tribune-Herald*'s opening shot, Waco was a classic American cult story, driven by atrocity stories from former members who told of unholy sex, fanatic devotion, and incomprehensible subservience to a charismatic patriarch. *Newsweek* in particular offered the full treatment inside its March 15 cover, "Secrets of the Cult." In addition to covering the events and group at hand, the magazine supplied the context in a who-joins-a-cult story headlined "From Prophets to Losses" and an article on "Cultic America" that began, "Waco is a wake-up call."

In time-honored tradition, the sexual aspects of the story became prime media fodder. Again, *Newsweek* could barely contain itself: "Young girls and old women, innocent and worldly, virginal and fecund. Within the walls of his kingdom on the flat plains of Texas, David Koresh knew them all—in the Biblical sense, former followers say." Younger and younger grew Koresh's "wives," the titillated magazine disclosed, such that eventually more than a dozen "nubile members of the flock succumbed."[25] The *Globe* supermarket tabloid did it a lot quicker on March 23 with "Mad Messiah Had Sex with Me and My Mom." Whether Koresh was actually guilty of a sex crime (such as statutory rape) seemed beside the point.

The allegations of child abuse centered on reports of corporal punishment and other strict disciplinary procedures. After the FBI assault incinerated the compound and most of its inhabitants, Attorney General Janet Reno even cited ongoing child abuse to explain the action, but no evidence of such abuse was subsequently brought forward. In fact, the first newspaper stories told how Texas social workers had previously inspected the compound and found insufficient grounds to justify removing the children—a revelation that, among other things, called into question the need for ATF's military-style tactics. (If a social worker could gain ready access to the compound, why not an ATF inspection team?) In short, as a justification for moving against the Branch Davidians, the charge of child abuse remained highly am-biguous. The child angle was, of course, central to coverage after the final conflagration, from editorialists' sober laments over the innocent dead to *Newsweek*'s May 17 background cover story, "Children of the Cult," to the *Globe*'s "Koresh Sacrificed Kids—So He'd Live Again." As the *Columbus* [Ga.] *Leader-Enquirer* put it, "That among the vic-tims of such false prophets are little children is almost more than the human heart can bear or the mind understand." [26]

What was left by way of justification was the putative reason the ATF had gotten involved in the first place: the Branch Davidians' alleged violation of federal firearms laws. Although the fire destroyed most of the evidence, there was little doubt that the group had pos-sessed grenades, fully automatic weapons, and other illegal military hardware. (Whether they had any plans to use the arsenal—except defensively against assault by imagined forces of darkness—was an unanswered question.) The need for stricter gun laws was a theme taken up by many editorial pages, among them the *Los Angeles Times*, which declared on April 20 that Congress must "take a fresh look at federal gun-control laws to close loopholes that allowed religious ex-tremists to become so heavily armed that they were able to first beat back, and then hold off, a small army for more than 50 days." With equal fervor, columnist (and former Reagan administration official) Paul Craig Roberts turned the criticism on its head and blamed the tragedy on the violation of the Davidians' Second Amendment right to bear arms: "Except for the federal gun laws, they would still be alive today." [27] Somehow, though, transmuting the Branch Davidian story into a gun control debate didn't seem to get to the heart of the matter, which was: Who was to blame for what happened?

Editorial opinion was divided. In a compilation of sixty-five edito-rials nationwide, the American Political Network's *Hotline* found that twenty singled out Koresh for blame, thirty-two took the federal gov-ernment to task, and thirteen praised Attorney General Reno (often in contrast to President Clinton) for coming out and shouldering re-sponsibility for the disastrous denouement. Media commentary is, of course, largely in business to criticize the government for one thing or another, and in this case there were ample grounds for criticism. Why did the ATF insist on rushing in? Why didn't the FBI wait Koresh out? Why can't the government figure out how to handle religious fanatics?

In all the criticism, however, there was a notable lack of attention to the free-exercise clause of the First Amendment, other than in the occasional op-ed piece by a religious-studies expert.[28] Of the dead Branch Davidians, Molly Ivins asked in her syndicated column, "What did they ever do to anyone?" Of dozens of editorials and columns reviewed, only the *Orange County Register* focused clearly on the First Amendment principles at stake, arguing on April 20 that the unwillingness of the ATF to forego its raid "bespeaks a government increasingly, and chillingly, estranged from a constitutional republic designed to tolerate religious eccentrics and political nuisances."

In line with the fond illusions of latter-day conservative populism, the *Register* suggested that "ordinary people" understood the need to tolerate such eccentrics far better than Big Brother, but there was little evidence of that. Rather than hold the authorities responsible, most Americans fixed blame squarely on the false prophet himself. According to an ABC poll taken in the wake of the destruction of the compound, 58 percent of respondents approved of the ATF's initial raid, while 76 percent blamed the Davidians for the ensuing shootout. An NBC poll taken at the same time showed two-thirds approval of the FBI assault on the compound, while in a Gallup poll 73 percent said the FBI acted responsibly and 93 percent blamed Koresh for the outcome.[29]

Nor, indeed, did the news media's coverage of Waco elicit the concern of the bias police. As noted earlier, the conservative Media Research Center excluded Waco stories (other than a few on the Davidians' religion) from its survey of religion news on network television. Part of the reason, doubtless, was that the sheer weight of the coverage would have indicated far more attention to religion than the survey was designed to show. Equally, however, the survey aimed to demonstrate a liberal, secular bias against conservative religious values. Making sure that marginal religious groups got fair coverage was not on its agenda. Neither did the middle-of-the-road Dart-Allen study of religion and the news media offer any recommendations regarding coverage of marginal religious groups. The study's only mention of the Davidian story came in a quotation from the historian Yvonne Haddad, who contrasted the media's treatment of Islam and Christianity. "We don't talk about Christianity as a religion of violence because there's a crazy man in Waco," she said.[30] In sum, if such observers declined to criticize the media's portrayal of David Koresh and his followers, it can only be because they found it in accord with their own religiously informed point of view.

To be sure, some in the organized religious community did worry about the impact of the Waco story. A couple of weeks after the disaster, a coalition of religious and civil liberties groups, including the National Council of Churches, the National Association of Evangelicals, and the American Civil Liberties Union, issued a statement urging the federal government not to use the affair as the occasion for holding hearings on cults: "History teaches that today's 'cults' may become tomorrow's mainstream religions. In the midst of our national mourning, we must fend off any inclination to shrink from our commitment to religious pluralism or to seek security at the expense of liberty. . . . Under the religious liberty provision of the First Amendment, government has no business declaring what is orthodox or heretical, or what is a true or false religion."[31] But this was the voice of the same folks who were battling in relative isolation for the Religious Freedom Restoration Act. Their concern did not appear to extend to the rest of the population.

In due course, heads rolled at ATF. And early in 1994, eleven surviving adult Branch Davidians went on trial for murder and conspiracy in the case of the four federal agents who died during the February 28 raid. Prosecutors had the job of persuading the jury that the defendants were people responsible for their actions, not brainwashed automatons. Defense attorneys represented their clients as victims of the "delusional," "paranoid" Koresh.[32] In the end, four were acquitted and seven found guilty of the lesser offenses of manslaughter and illegal-weapons possession. But the country showed little interest in the denouement of the story that had occupied center stage for two months the previous year. The false prophet was dead, and it hardly seemed to matter any more.

NOTES

1. Leonard J. Arrington and Davis Bitton, *The Mormon Experience: A History of the Latter-day Saints,* 2d ed. (Urbana: University of Illinois Press,

1992), 72–82. Perhaps symbolically, it was the church's suppression of an anti-Mormon newspaper founded in Nauvoo by a group of dissidents that precipitated the assassination of its founder, Joseph Smith, and his followers' departure west.

2. Jan Shipps, "From Satyr to Saint: American Attitudes toward the Mormons," typescript of paper presented at the 1973 annual meeting of the Organization of American Historians, 6.

3. Gustive O. Larson, *The "Americanization" of Utah for Statehood* (San Marino: Huntington Library, 1971), 53–54.

4. Horace Greeley, *An Overland Journey from New York to San Francisco in the Summer of 1859* (New York: Alfred A. Knopf, 1964), 205, 213. For an account of the various journalists who called on Brigham Young, see Leonard J. Arrington, *Brigham Young: American Moses* (New York: Alfred A. Knopf, 1985), ch. 18.

5. Greeley, *An Overland Journey*, 182, 213.

6. On the campaign against the Oneida community, with excerpts of press reaction, see Robert Allerton Parker, *A Yankee Saint: John Humphrey Noyes and the Oneida Community* (New York: Putnam's, 1935; Philadelphia: Porcupine Press, 1972), 267–83.

7. "Let any such system become established and prevalent, and woman will soon be confined to the harem, and her appearance in the street with unveiled face will be accounted immodest. I joyfully trust that the genius of the nineteenth century tends to a solution of the problem of woman's sphere and destiny radically different from this." Greeley, *An Overland Journey*, 185.

8. Shipps, "From Satyr to Saint," 18, 19.

9. Paul E. Johnson and Sean Wilentz, *The Kingdom of Matthias: A Story of Sex and Salvation in Nineteenth-Century America* (New York: Oxford University Press, 1994), 173. The authors note that the penny press seemed as concerned with Matthias as with the great issues of slavery and abolitionism that consume the attention of historians of Jacksonian America (146). If the story of Matthias's Kingdom—like the story of the Mormons—really was about patriarchy and the status of women, then perhaps the newspapers knew what they were doing, at least unconsciously.

10. *Reynolds v. United States*, 98 U.S. 145.

11. Barry van Driel and Jacob van Belzen, "The Downfall of Rajneeshpuram: A Cross-National Study," *Journal for the Scientific Study of Religion* 29, no. 1 (1990): 76–90.

12. Ron Lovell, "Dissecting a Sect," *The Quill* 74 (May 1986): 16, 15.

13. A psychological study of members of the Rajneesh commune found that they ranked high in self-esteem and private self-consciousness, findings that tend to contradict the conventional image of "cult" members as malleable victims. See Carl A. Latkin, "The Self-Concept of Rajneeshpuram

Commune Members," *Journal for the Scientific Study of Religion* 29, no. 1 (1990): 91–98.

14. Barend van Driel and James T. Richardson, "Print Media Coverage of New Religious Movements: A Longitudinal Study," *Journal of Communication* 38 (Summer 1988): 37–61.

15. Thomas Robbins and Dick Anthony, "Deprogramming, Brainwashing and the Medicalization of Deviant Religious Groups," *Social Problems* 29 (February 1982): 290, 293.

16. Robbins and Anthony, "Deprogramming," 284.

17. On the image of communism as a religion during the cold war, see Mark Silk, *Spiritual Politics: Religion and America since World War II* (New York: Simon and Schuster, 1988), 88–97.

18. To the extent that the concept of brainwashing draws on cultural stereotypes of the Far East (opium addiction, the hypnotic stare of Fu Manchu), this may not be such a coincidence after all.

19. David G. Bromley, Anson D. Shupe, Jr., and J. C. Ventimiglia, "Atrocity Tales, the Unification Church, and the Social Construction of Evil," *Journal of Communication* 29 (Summer 1979): 46, 53. Although van Driel and Richardson have questioned whether this study meets the strict methodological standards of content analysis, their own work confirms its underlying claim of the media's general hostility to new religious movements. They argue, moreover, that in portraying new religious movements as being at odds with American society, "print media reporting reflects the prevailing attitudes of the wider society." Van Driel and Richardson, "Print Media," 51–55.

20. Ibid., 57–58.

21. For the use of "cult" as a term of opprobrium, see Barend van Driel and James T. Richardson, "Categorization of New Religious Movements in American Print Media," *Sociological Analysis* 49, no. 2 (1988): 171–83. As the authors disconsolately conclude, "A great deal of effort has been expended within the social-scientific tradition to unravel the complexities of marginal religious organizations. Unfortunately it seems that the message is somehow totally lost to the majority of those employed by the major print media" (182).

22. The *Times* did not, however, attempt to put Scientology in any larger religious context. Sidney Alstrom, in his standard account of religion in America, identifies Scientology as part of the psychology-influenced "peace of mind" spiritual wave that broke over American society after World War II. See *A Religious History of the American People* (New Haven: Yale University Press, 1972), 955n. For all the eccentricity of its cosmology, Scientology would seem to fit snugly within the long tradition of American mind-cure first sketched out by William James in Lectures 4 and 5 of *The Varieties of Religious Experience*. Historical context is not the news media's strong suit, for in general it tends to detract from the distinctiveness (and hence newsworthiness)

of any subject. In this case, it would tend to undermine Scientology's long-standing image of threat and deviance. See, for example, Eugene H. Methvin, "Scientology: Anatomy of a Frightening Cult," *Reader's Digest* (May 1980): 86–91. In the words of one observer, "The nature of the debate surrounding Scientology, and some of the rhetoric that has appeared during its course, suggest that at times Scientology has been viewed in a manner approaching *moral panic.*" Roy Wallis, "Societal Reaction to Scientology: A Study in the Sociology of Deviant Religion," in *Sectarianism,* ed. Wallis (London: Peter Owen, 1975), 86.

23. *Time* (March 15, 1993), 24.

24. *Tribune-Herald,* February 27, 1993 (editorial); March 1, 1993 (admission of knowledge of the imminent ATF raid). The newspaper was accused of rushing its series into print early lest ATF action rob it of its righteous anger (and a chance at a Pulitzer Prize) by Wendell Rawls in "Debacle at Waco," *Nieman Reports* 47 (Summer 1993): 14–15. In the NBC docudrama "In the Line of Duty: Ambush in Waco," which he researched and produced, Rawls put the charge in the mouth of an ATF agent ("Who'd start a series on Saturday?") in the course of apportioning a considerable part of the blame for the botched raid to the newspaper. The "irresponsible media" topos also appeared in charges by some observers that sensationalistic coverage put unnecessary pressure on the FBI to bring the standoff to an end.

25. *Newsweek,* March 15, 1993, 56.

26. *Globe,* May 4, 1993. (Alternatively, the *Star* chose a cover story on "Waco's Little Angel"—a sixteen-year-old "Hellfire survivor.") *Leader-Enquirer,* April 22, 1993.

27. Scripps Howard News Service, April 21, 1993.

28. For example, Mary Zeiss Stange, associate professor of religion at Skidmore College, wrote in the *Los Angeles Times* (AP wire, April 20, 1993): "I am in no way defending Koresh or his views; indeed, what he practiced and preached is repellent to me. But it is religion—in fact, religion of a not-uncommon type in our society. Prattling on about thought control and de-programming, profiling its leader as a nut case and his followers as social misfits does not alter that fact." A few members of the working press wrote pieces pointing out that eccentric religious groups have been common throughout American history. See Karl E. Meyer, " 'Cults,' Deconstructed," *New York Times,* March 7, 1993.

29. Associated Press, April 22, 1993; *New York Times,* April 25, 1993.

30. John Dart and Jimmy Allen, *Bridging the Gap: Religion and the News Media* (Nashville: Freedom Forum First Amendment Center, 1993), 31.

31. Religious New Service, May 5, 1993.

32. *New York Times,* February 26, 1994.

CHAPTER NINE

Inclusion

Where there is neither Greek nor Jew, circumcision
nor uncircumcision, Barbarian, Scythian, bond nor
free. . . .

COLOSSIANS 3:11

"You are a Jew in America. Correction: You are an American who
happens to be Jewish. (The distinction is important, as we'll see.)" So
begins *Look* magazine's November 29, 1955, cover story, "The Position
of the Jews in America Today." Cast in catechetical form (What is a
Jew? How are Jews different from other Americans?), it offers a classic
example of the topos of religious inclusion, in which a suspect faith
is shown to be composed of good Americans worshipping according
to their own worthy lights.

    William Attwood, the magazine's national affairs editor and a self-
described Gentile, tells how he has traveled around the country and
found that Jews are temperate, industrious, devoted to family, zealous
for education, generous, and endowed with good senses of humor.
They also, he reports, have smaller crime, divorce, delinquency, and
alcoholism rates than the population at large and more college graduates. Judaism itself turns out to be an ethical faith more concerned
with behavior in this world than with what happens in the here-
after. An accompanying photo essay depicts a typical American Jewish
family at work, at play, and celebrating Hanukkah at home in the typical American town of Flint, Michigan. There is also a photo lineup of
Jews who have made important contributions to American life: Jonas
Salk, Hank Greenberg, Saul Bellow, Kirk Douglas, etc. Attwood makes
no bones about the persistence of anti-Semitism in American society,

especially in social clubs and corporate boardrooms. The explanation? "Ignorance plus fear creates prejudice." But anti-Semitism is on the wane, more an "irritant" than a bar to success.

The article celebrates not only the Jews but also America itself, whose welcome makes it the only country in the Diaspora they are prepared to call home. To the final question—Will Jews ever be completely integrated in America?—Attwood answers yes as to equal social and economic status, but no as to their maintaining a separate Jewish identity. Why shouldn't they remain Jews? Borrowing from Will Herberg's recently published *Protestant Catholic Jew,* he avers that religious distinctions are the only ones that survive in American society, and that being identified as a member of the Jewish faith will ultimately be recognized as an assertion of a Jew's Americanism. The journalist is not unconscious of his own part in the process: "I venture to say that in another generation, there will be no purpose in a report such as this one." Demystifying and applauding the American Jewish community for the benefit of an American mass audience would simply cease to be necessary.[1]

It is no accident that such an article should have appeared at this time. Hitler's destruction of European Jewry had seriously undermined the respectability of domestic anti-Semitism, which was assailed in such popular entertainments as the best-selling novel and feature film *Gentleman's Agreement.* Moreover, World War II and then the cold war had seemed to require a common American religious creed, to which end the term *Judeo-Christian* was pressed into service.[2] A Judeo-Christian civilization could not in good faith discriminate against Jews, nor were they the only ones to benefit from the need for a united religious front against totalitarianism. It was during the same period that the LDS church was fully brought into the fold of national media acceptability, notably by *Reader's Digest,* which published no fewer than seven appreciative articles about Mormons between 1937 and 1958.[3]

But grand ideological struggle is hardly a prerequisite for the topos of inclusion, which hovers like a benign spirit over any routine coverage of a minority faith. The mere taking note of a festival or rite serves a legitimating function—saying, in effect, here is another authentic religious body whose activities enrich the community at large. Such coverage is a natural function of newspapers, which seek to appeal to all segments of the reading community. It plays an essential role in

constructing groups that once seemed threatening into the comfortable institutional furniture of society. As noted in the last chapter, at
the height of cult anxiety in the 1970s the press never leveled charges
of brainwashing or manipulation at familiar unconventional religious
bodies like Jehovah's Witnesses and Christian Science, but concerned
itself rather with explaining their beliefs, thereby rendering them com-
prehensible and acceptable to readers.[4] Call it the domestication of
eccentricity.

The acceptance of alien faiths, if not always on their own terms,
comes easily in a country that has enshrined in national myth its identity as a place of refuge for the religiously persecuted. What could be
more American than coming to America in order to be able to worship
at the church of your choice? But just as the inclusion topos draws its
strength from ambient Americanism, so its anti-topos is foreignness.
What made Catholics traditionally suspect was their alleged subservience to a foreign power; as late as the 1980s, Protestant groups opposed President Ronald Reagan's decision to recognize that power by
sending an ambassador to the Vatican. Eastern religious leaders from
the Bhagwan Shree Rajneesh to the Rev. Sun Myung Moon were seen
not just as false prophets but as outsiders threatening pious Americans
with strange fire. Even an indigenous new religion like Mormonism
was assailed in the nineteenth century on account of its large number
of foreign adherents.

The inclusion topos is primarily for domestic use. Thus, when the
locus of public attention lies not with American adherents but with
their co-religionists abroad, the topos may be undermined—at least
as far as the members of the faith are concerned—by other topoi that
come into play. In the case of the Jews, the foreign locus has, since
1948, been the state of Israel. The only hint of a reservation Attwood
expresses about the place of Jews in American society shows up in his
answer to the question of whether a U.S. Jew could support the state
of Israel and still be a good American. He can answer, he says, "without any equivocation" that there is "no divided loyalty on the part of
American Jews." But after cautioning his readers not to underestimate
either the "affinity" of nearly all Jews for Israel or their (American)
patriotism, he adds:

> The leaders of certain Jewish organizations have been so carried
> away by their enthusiasm for Israel that they raise a hullabaloo
> each time American foreign policy seems to conflict with that of

Israel. Fortunately, I found many responsible leaders concerned about this; among the rank-and-file Jews I talked with, most of them readily made the distinction between financial aid to a struggling, pioneer nation and blind support of the policies of what is, after all, a foreign power.[5]

It is fair to say that the image of a struggling, pioneer nation beset by large and powerful foes dominated media coverage of Israel for the first two decades of its existence. Then, with the 1967 Six-Day War, the topos of the deserving underdog begin to shift. Military triumph, the peacemaking initiative of the Egyptian leader Anwar Sadat, Israel's 1982 invasion of Lebanon, and above all the uprising of Palestinians in the occupied territories of Gaza and the West Bank all helped create a more complex and less favorable portrait of the Jewish state. Israel now appeared to be the most powerful country in the region, capable of throwing its weight around militarily and occupying lands populated by large Arab majorities. For their part, the Arabs were no longer simply implacable, prejudiced enemies but, as Palestinians, victims in their own right fighting for self-determination.[6]

Within the American Jewish community, the shift from nearly unalloyed journalistic approval of Israel created considerable distress. The Anti-Defamation League of B'nai B'rith, the community's prejudice watchdog agency, began focusing attention on media coverage of events in the Middle East. In the wake of the Lebanon invasion, for example, the ADL issued a report charging the television networks with lack of balance for reporting inflated casualty figures and failing to put the event into perspective. Documentaries such as PBS's 1989 "Days of Rage: The Young Palestinians" and a 1990 "Sixty Minutes" segment on the killings at the Temple Mount in Jerusalem also elicited ADL critiques. When NBC's "Today" show did a sympathetic story on the Palestinians in February 1991, ADL director Abraham Foxman wrote an angry letter to the show's executive producer, denouncing the presentation of the Israeli-Palestinian conflict "as a black and white issue with Israel the brutal oppressor and the Palestinians the innocent victims of Israeli aggression."[7] In addition to such remonstrations from the Jewish establishment, there issued less restrained attacks from a new organization, the Committee for Accuracy in Middle East Reporting in America (CAMERA). With chapters around the country, CAMERA kept close watch on local newspapers as well as national Middle East reporting, singling out for particular opprobrium the

Boston Globe, CBS's Mike Wallace, ABC's Peter Jennings, and Linda Gradstein of National Public Radio.[8]

What accounted for the media's apparently newfound bias against Israel? At a CAMERA national conference held in Boston in 1989, a variety of explanations were offered. Ruth Wisse, professor of Jewish studies at McGill University, explained it in terms of the transformation of Jews "from a nation of victims to a nation of villains." Former ambassador Alan Keyes, asking why the media should "sign on to an underlying desire to destroy Israel," pointed to the evolution of the Middle East story from peace, security, and war into a "human rights paradigm" with Israel as violator. Wellesley College history professor Jerold Auerbach blamed critical coverage in the Jewish-owned *New York Times* on the *Times*'s "prolonged Jewish identity problem." But, as the Boston *Jewish Advocate* pointed out on November 2, only David Wyman, the non-Jewish author of *The Abandonment of the Jews,* "dared to make a charge that none of the Jewish speakers did"—that anti-Semitism lay at the heart of the "media bias": "The people in the media would not personally mistreat a Jew. But beneath the surface, unconscious and uncrystallized, there is a definite negativity toward Jews that is deeply engrained in Western society. Almost all non-Jews are infected, but each of us can confront that and subdue it."

Jews were, to be sure, capable of linking hostility to Israel with anti-Semitism, which in various quarters marched under the banner of anti-Zionism. But issuing blanket charges of anti-Semitism against the American news media, even in Wyman's attenuated form, was something else again. In 1982, the ADL's Nathan Perlmutter and his wife Ruth Ann wrote a tract defining anti-Semitism as whatever impaired the real interests of Jews. By that definition, critical news coverage of Israel could be deemed ipso facto anti-Semitic. But like other neo-conservative intellectuals, the Perlmutters seemed mainly interested in persuading American Jews to abandon their customary liberal sympathies in favor of Reaganite conservatism. In a long article reviewing anti-Semitic writings of novelist Gore Vidal (on the Left) and journalist Joe Sobran (on the Right), *Commentary* magazine's Norman Podhoretz came to the conclusion that anti-Semitism "has largely if not entirely been banished from its traditional home on the Right, and that today, especially in the guise of anti-Zionism, it is meeting with more and more toleration, and sometimes even approval, on the Left."[9]

In line with the Lichter and Rothman portrayal of the media elite, those criticizing the media for anti-Israeli bias tended to separate journalistic attitudes from those of the American public at large. For their part, the Perlmutters dismissed the thought that Christian anti-Semitism in any way threatened Jewish life in America and urged an entente with the Christian Right.[10] In a study of coverage of the Palestinian uprising, Eytan Gilboa of the Hebrew University discovered that the American news media offered a considerably more balanced picture than partisans in the American Jewish community imagined; but to the limited extent that coverage was skewed against Israel, Gilboa found it to be out of step with public opinion.[11] Inasmuch as Middle East coverage expressed the views of the media elite, it could be taxed, at most, with fashionable anti-Semitic fellow-traveling.

In any event, the entire issue of liberal media bias against Israel began to lose altitude in the 1990s. The willingness of Israel to suffer Iraqi missile attacks without striking back during the 1991 Gulf War helped revive the image of the Jewish state's vulnerability. More important, the abandonment of aggressive settlement policies by a new Labor government, followed by its 1993 peace agreement with the Palestinians, went some way toward restoring Israel's peace-loving credentials. Meanwhile, the postcommunist revival of anti-Semitism in the former Eastern bloc gave the lie to the neoconservative reassessment of where hostility to the Jews lay—as did the anti-Semitic wisecracks and anti-Israel pronouncements of conservative pundit and 1992 Republican presidential aspirant Pat Buchanan. At the same time, ugly anti-Semitic diatribes by radical black leaders gave the media plenty of opportunity to demonstrate its hostility to anti-Jewish prejudice on the Left.

In short, the more critical perspective on Israel in the 1970s and 1980s appears to have been just that and no more. Even at the height of Jewish concern, American Jews were reluctant to charge the media with outright anti-Semitism. Their inclusion in American society was too well established to be threatened seriously by coverage of Jews abroad. By contrast, during the same period Muslim Americans faced a society deeply suspicious of their religious faith.

In Western European culture generally, Muhammad was the false prophet par excellence; from the Crusades to the near sack of eighteenth-century Vienna, Muslims had been those whom Christians fought against. In the United States, however, Islam histori-

cally attracted little attention. Traces of the religion can be found
in nineteenth-century America, from the war against the Barbary
pirates to Mark Twain's travel books. American missionaries doubtless brought back images of the faith. But most actual immigrants
to America from Muslim countries were Christians from Syria and
Lebanon. Although, at the end of the twentieth century, American Muslims numbered several million (estimates varied considerably), the most salient Islamic group remains the Nation of Islam,
the black separatist religion that came to national notice during
civil rights era. At that time, the Nation (in the persons of Elijah
Muhammad and Malcolm X) represented a spiritual antithesis of the
integrationist civil-rights ministries of Martin Luther King, Jr., and
other African-American Christian activists. Determinedly outside the
Judeo-Christian pale, it was portrayed as what lay in wait for a society
that failed to do right by its black citizens.[12]

Abroad, Islam cut a relatively low profile as well.[13] Whereas Israel
was recognized from the outset as an expression of religious aspira-
tions, it was not until the 1978 Iranian revolution that its adversaries
began to be seen in Muslim, as opposed to Arab nationalist, terms.
Time's cover story of April 16, 1979, "The Militant Revival," and "Militant Islam: The Historic Whirlwind" in the January 6, 1980, *New York
Times Magazine* were just two of innumerable accounts of an Islamic
revival that conjured up images of the original Muslim conquests: a
scimitar of holy war slashing a wide "arc of crisis" through the oil-rich
belly of the world. With the seizure of the American embassy in Tehran
by students in November 1979 and the year-long drama that followed,
a religion that few Americans knew anything about turned into a
national bogey. In 1981, the British journalist Edward Mortimer could
write, "The main difference in our perception today is that whereas
we never dreamed such a thing could happen in Iran we are now constantly on the lookout for it in every Muslim country. Where before
Islam was largely ignored, now it is seen everywhere, even where it
has no particular relevance."[14]

Edward Said, the Palestinian literary scholar, blamed academic experts and the media together for creating a public image of Islam "in a
confrontational relationship with whatever is normal, Western, everyday, 'ours.'"[15] Certainly, the portrait of Islam-on-the-march tended
to limit increased sympathy for the Palestinians in the Israeli-Arab
conflict. (To some on the Arab side, the sympathy seemed minimal

at best.)[16] American foreign policy was Islamically confused, tilting toward secularist Iraq in the Iran-Iraq war, supporting Islamic freedom fighters against the Soviet puppet regime in Afghanistan, maintaining traditional ties to the "conservative" Islamic states of the Persian Gulf, then going to war against Iraq on their behalf. The determining issues, of course, were oil and geopolitics, not religion.

Here is not the place to rehearse the catalog of horrors with which Said and other Muslim sympathizers have indicted the American media for their portrayal of Islam. Instead, I want to explore the dynamics of inclusion that played themselves out in the pages of the *Atlanta Journal-Constitution* and other newspapers in the early 1990s.

On June 28, 1992, the *Journal-Constitution* published a special twelve-page section, "Women of the Veil," that sought to show how "Islamic militants" were "pushing women back to an age of official servitude." The report was the outcome of a six-week tour through Turkey, Pakistan, Afghanistan, and Kuwait by reporter Deborah Scroggins and photographer Jean Shifrin. In a feat reminiscent of the undercover tours of Arabia by nineteenth-century European adventurers, the two journalists donned veils to explore the world of Muslim women.[17] The motivation for the series was the Gulf War, in which the contrast was striking between American female military personnel working alongside men to liberate Kuwait and Saudi Arabian women who were not allowed to drive an automobile. "We had just gone to war to preserve this way of life," recalled Robert Lee Hotz, the newspaper's projects editor, in July 1993 by way of explanation.

The headlines were fairly sensational: "Male Honor Costs Women's Lives," "Imprisoned for Love," "Using Rape to Settle Scores," "To Protect Chastity, Some Practice Mutilation." Excerpts from the Koran were printed to demonstrate the religious basis for the legal subordination of women. "The liberty of women," the lead article declared, "is the first casualty in the Islamic counter-revolution." This portrait of oppression was leavened somewhat by articles on educated Muslim women who favored the veil and Muslim feminists who found koranic justification for equal status. It was also pointed out, in a short article at the bottom of page 9, that "American Muslims, like many non-American Muslims, oppose the idea of forcing people to obey their religion." But overall, the portrait was of a faith profoundly hostile to what "we" stand for. Thus: "Islam admits no separation of mosque and state." And: "With the demise of communism, Islamic fundamentalism has become the only organized, international rallying point for opposition to the West. And what drives the fury, in part, is the fear that the Western emphasis on individual rights is destroying Islamic family values."

Reaction was swift and furious. The newspaper received almost a thousand telephone calls and seventy-five letters, many from Muslims outraged at the series. Two pages of reader reaction (not all critical) were printed, as well as an article attacking the "ignorant stereotype that Islam itself [as opposed to 'socio-historical conditions'] denigrates women" by Fadwa El Gundi, an anthropologist specializing in Islamic feminism.[18] In addition, delegations of local Muslims came to the newspaper to complain that the "true Islam" had been misrepresented and insulted.

"I was surprised at the degree to which the American Muslim community saw this being directly about them, even though we tried to be expressly about the heart of Islam — the Mediterranean rim," Hotz said. "We were naive. Probably we should have made the disclaimer more prominent." Hotz did not back away from the report's accuracy, or the newspaper's right to criticize a religion. "We thought, 'We're not talking about someone's religion as a private practice. We're talking about political religion.' All these countries are signatories to human rights treaties requiring equality for women. At some point you do stand on your culture. We have placed a value on the status of women." Yet, he concluded, "What more volatile topic is there than religion? To write about it seriously and aggressively is to court disaster. You're also writing about communities. There's that sense of assault on community virtue."

As far as the *Journal-Constitution*'s approach to Islam was concerned, however, "Women of the Veil" stood out against the trend of coverage. For a decade, the newspaper had been giving increasing, respectful attention to Muslims as part of the American scene. Thus, Ramadan, the month-long period of atonement, gained a niche in the catalog of holidays acknowledged in the religion, food, and general news pages. In the five years between 1985 and 1989, there were nine references to Ramadan as celebrated by Muslims in America; in the following five-year period, the number grew to twenty-two. After the Ayatollah Khomeini issued his *fatwa* against the British-Pakistani author Salman Rushdie, the newspaper ran a story on February 25,

1989 about local Muslim opposition to the ayatollah's action. It was not, said the imam of an Atlanta mosque, "the Islamic way." On June 8, a feature story on Islam as America's fastest-growing religion began: "Say the word Muslim, and many white Americans think 'Arab terrorist.' 'Neighbor' would be a more accurate term." So it was in keeping with the pattern of coverage that, after an Atlanta man was arrested in connection with the World Trade Center bombing, the author of "Women of the Veil" and another reporter addressed the situation of the local Muslim community in a story headlined, "Muslims caught in the middle: Atlanta worshipers say America's view of Islam focuses on a few fanatics." Atlanta's ten thousand Muslims were, they wrote, "increasingly prosperous and ethnically diverse," but feel "sadly misunderstood by many of their fellow citizens." [19]

The pattern of using news that seemed to reflect badly on Muslims as a peg for stories with an inclusion topos was not confined to the *Journal-Constitution*. On April 6, 1993, a month after the Trade Center bombing, the *Los Angeles Times* published a long special report, "Islam Rising," which offered a balanced and carefully differentiated portrait of Islam around the world. The story about Muslims in the United States, "Muslims Enter American Mainstream," was a parable of ethnic assimilation. The torch was being passed, said the newspaper, to a new, politically savvy, middle-class generation "with concerns that are as representative of America as an Aaron Copeland suite"—a nicely calculated image extended in the assertion that Muslim Americans were as enthusiastic for a Palestinian state as Jewish Americans had been for a Jewish state in 1948. Not surprisingly, among the Muslims' concerns was the difficulty of preserving their religious and cultural heritage while fitting into the mainstream.

A few weeks later, the *New York Times* published its own four-part series on Muslims in America, which centered on the familiar theme of immigrants "eager to adapt but at the same time retain a separate religious identity"—an identity incorporating moral values much like those of other Americans. As for the large number of African-American Muslims, they were, mutatis mutandis, entering the Islamic mainstream. An article on the establishment of a new mosque ended with the typically American religious remark of an Orthodox rabbi who came to the ceremony to show his support: "This spirit of cooperation is what we have to export to other countries.[20] Both the *Los*

Angeles Times and the *New York Times* emphasized Muslims' anger
and concern that "extremists" could create the impression that Islam
was a religion of fanaticism.

To cite one more example, after anti-Semitic remarks by a spokesman for the Nation of Islam set off a storm of criticism in early 1994,
USA Today on January 27 published a special report on Islam in the
United States. Again, the emphasis was on what Islam shares "with
America's dominant Judeo-Christian culture, with its emphasis on
family, work and tolerance." Again, the goal of Muslims was assimilation, but not at the cost of religious identity. In a sidebar, "mainstream
Muslim groups" were quoted condemning the spokesman's remarks
as contrary to Islam.

One of the recommendations of the 1993 Dart-Allen study of religion and the news media was for an academic study of Islam and
Muslims to determine the actual extent of media bias.[21] By then, however, news organizations were clearly taking pains to portray Islam
as a wholesome American faith. Their recourse to the inclusion topos
doubtless reflected some recognition of the growing numbers of Muslims in their circulation areas, as well as a desire to quiet the concerns
of this increasingly vocal Muslim community. But the media also appeared to be repenting of the sins of the past.

NOTES

1. William Attwood, "The Position of the Jews in America Today," *Look*,
November 29, 1955, 27–35. A generation later, a major article on "the Jews"
would take the form of the *Los Angeles Times*' January 1992 state-of-the-
community report that detailed anxieties about recurrent anti-Semitism,
hostility to Israel, high rates of intermarriage, and low rates of reproduction.

2. See Mark Silk, "Notes on the Judeo-Christian Tradition in America,"
American Quarterly 36 (Spring 1984): 65–85; also Silk, *Spiritual Politics: Religion and America since World War II* (New York: Simon and Schuster, 1988),
40–53.

3. See Jan Shipps, "From Satyr to Saint: American Attitudes toward the
Mormons," typescript of paper presented at the 1973 annual meeting of the
Organization of American Historians, 37.

4. Barend van Driel and James T. Richardson, "Print Media Coverage of
New Religious Movements: A Longitudinal Study," *Journal of Communication*
38 (Summer 1988): 37–61.

5. Attwood, "The Position of the Jews," 30.

6. The shifts in media images of the Arab-Israeli conflict can be traced in the following studies: Janice Monti Belkaoui, "Images of Arabs and Israelis in the Prestige Press," *Journalism Quarterly* 55 (Winter 1978): 732–38, 799; Janice Terry and Gordon Mendenhall, "1973 U.S. Press Coverage on the Middle East," *Journal of Palestine Studies* 4, no. 1 (1974): 120–33; Morad Osman Asi, "Arabs, Israelis and U.S. Television Network: A Content Analysis of How ABC, CBS, and NBC Reported the News between 1970–1979," Ph.D. diss., Ohio University, 1981, *Dissertation Abstract International* 42, 436A–37A; Nabiha Habbab Ghandour, "Coverage of the Arab World and Israel in American News Magazines between 1975 and 1981: A Comparative Content Analysis," Ph.D. diss., Teachers College of Columbia University, 1984, *Dissertation Abstract International* 45, 2476A; Manny Paraschos and Bill Rutherford, "Network News Coverage of Invasion of Lebanon by Israeli in 1982," *Journalism Quarterly* 62 (Autumn 1965): 457–64; Eytan Gilboa, "American Media Messages and Public Opinion on the Palestinian Uprising," *Political Communication and Persuasion* 6, no. 3 (1989): 191–202. In the 1983 version of his *Split Vision: The Portrayal of Arabs in the American Media* (Washington: American-Arab Affairs Council, 1983), Edmund Ghareeb could write, "Increased information has in some cases resulted in a more balanced approach to the region, less prone to distortion and bias. Many of the worst excesses associated with the portrayal of Arabs have been corrected" (157).

7. Anti-Defamation League of B'nai B'rith, "Television Network Coverage of the War in Lebanon" (New York, October 1982); reports on "Days of Rage" and "Sixty Minutes" segment, and February 21, 1991, letter from Foxman to Tom Capra of "Today," are from ADL files.

8. See, for example, "National Public Radio: A Study in News Manipulation," *CAMERA Media Report* 4 (Fall 1992): 1–14, 19.

9. Norman Podhoretz, "The Hate That Dare Not Speak Its Name," *Commentary* 82 (November 1986): 21–32.

10. Nathan Perlmutter and Ruth Ann Perlmutter, *The Real Anti-Semitism in America* (New York: Arbor House, 1982), 156, 172.

11. Gilboa, "American Media Messages," 195–99.

12. Silk, *Spiritual Politics*, 128–29.

13. For a critique of the West's inattention to the role of Islam on the world stage, see Bernard Lewis, "The Return of Islam," *Commentary* 61 (January 1976): 39–49.

14. Edward Mortimer, "Islam and the Western Journalist," *The Middle East Journal* 35 (Autumn 1981): 502.

15. Edward W. Said, *Covering Islam: How the Media and the Experts Determine How We See the Rest of the World* (New York: Pantheon, 1981), 39.

16. For a study of media coverage of the Israeli invasion of Lebanon wholly

at odds with the B'nai B'rith view, see Mary C. McDavid, "Media Myths of the Middle East: The U.S. Press on the War in Lebanon," in *Split Vision*, ed. Ghareeb, 299–313.

17. The point of view also had its roots in the nineteenth century. See chapter 8, note 7.

18. The reaction was published on June 30, July 5, and July 12.

19. *Atlanta Journal-Constitution*, March 24, 1993, August 22, 1993.

20. *New York Times*, May 2–4, 1993.

21. John Dart and Jimmy Allen, *Bridging the Gap: Religion and the News Media* (Nashville: Freedom Forum First Amendment Center, 1993), 64.

CHAPTER TEN

Supernatural
Belief

Now when he was in Jerusalem at the passover, in
the feast day, many believed in his name, when they
saw the miracles which he did.

JOHN 2:23

It is sometimes claimed that journalists have trouble with religion because they cannot cope professionally with matters that are beyond
empirical determination. As the former editor of the *Nashville Tennes-
sean,* John Siegenthaler, dramatically put it, the news media and religion are "two alien cultures—one rooted largely in a search for facts
and the other grounded in a discovery of faith beyond fact."[1] Whether
the two cultures are actually at such epistemological loggerheads is
open to question. Jesus, after all, gave his followers an empirical test
for distinguishing true prophets from false: "By their fruits ye shall
know them" (Matt. 7:20). As for news reporting, it often traffics in the
claims and beliefs of others. But if journalism has a religion "knowledge problem," it would seem to be most vexing in stories about the
supernatural—a category of being that, from an unbeliever's perspective, has nothing in it. What should a news organization do when it
receives word of a miraculous healing, an apparition of the Virgin
Mary, a poltergeist?

The simplest answer is: Let the word go forth. That is the approach
of the supermarket tabloids, where the supernatural is ensconced as
a regular item on the bill of bizarre and amazing fare. In the present
context, this coverage is worth our attention. The tabloids may be dis-

missed as disreputable purveyors of sleaze and untruth, but as S. Elizabeth Bird observes, they "cast themselves as guardians of a particular
kind of moral code that sits well with their regular readers."[2] The code
extends to traditional Judeo-Christian beliefs, and the papers make it
their business to report on signs and wonders that support these beliefs.

"Proof" stories are the specialty of the *Weekly World News*. In 1992,
for example, the *News*'s June 2 cover announced that the skeletons
of Adam and Eve had been unearthed in Colorado: "Amazing proof
Book of Genesis is true!" The September 15 cover featured the "first
photo of a human soul"—a ghostly, Blakean woman rising from an
operating table. "This is the proof that true believers the world over
have been waiting for," a German biblical scholar named Dr. Martin
Muller was quoted as saying. Similarly, on October 13 the cover story
was a photograph that purported to show Satan's face appearing in
the midst of Hurricane Andrew. "The photograph," said the story,
"has been hailed as proof positive that the devil exists and that it is
he who causes the world's disasters." A nonorthodox example of this
kind of coverage can be found in the June 8, 1993, number of another
tabloid, the *Sun*, which offered photographic proof of reincarnation
in the form of a two-headed baby, one of whose heads spoke medieval
English and the other, ancient Latin.

The secrets of holy texts particularly preoccupy the *Sun*, which on
November 5, 1991, picked up on the controversy over scholarly control
of the Dead Sea Scrolls by running a cover story on the scrolls' predictions of the future, including a cure for AIDS and the coming of a
latter-day prophet named Elvis. (The *News* followed suit on November 19, though with a different set of predictions, including the election of Caroline Kennedy to the presidency in 1996 following the second term of George Bush.) On December 17, 1991, the *Sun*'s annual
"Bible predictions" for the coming year had Magic Johnson ending the
AIDS crisis, a UFO bringing peace to the Middle East, and an earthquake shattering California. In its April 13, 1993, issue, the paper reported on the discovery of the Vatican's secret files on life after death.

The other staple of tabloid religious wonders are healing miracles,
usually conventional enough but occasionally as novel as the woman
who licked an Elvis stamp and was cured of throat cancer. ("He was a
gift from God," the *Sun* reported her saying on February 16, 1993. "I
definitely think they should make him a saint.") In its August 3, 1993,

issue, the *News* featured a special report on "miracles from around the world," which began with a "mind-numbing new survey" showing that 73 percent of Americans "have had life-altering experiences that cannot be explained by science." The miracles, "sure to make a believer out of the hardest of hearts," included a four-year-old cured of AIDS at Lourdes; a monk able to heal the sick and change the weather; a vision of Moses above an old apple tree; a "real-life flying nun" who floats in the air and heals the sick; a man who bleeds healing holy oil; the image of a dead patient's body on a hospital mattress; an out-of-body experience of a man whose heart stopped; the story of the tapestry cloak of the Virgin of Guadalupe; and advice about how saying the Lord's Prayer "literally can work a miracle in your life" (according to "experts in religion and psychology").

The tabloids are nothing if not attached to the rhetoric of objective empirical demonstration. A report in the June 8, 1993, *Sun* of three healing miracles accomplished through the Shroud of Turin emphasizes that scientists have found "more proof" of the shroud's authenticity as Jesus' burial cloth. "Stunning new scientific evidence" reveals that prayer *can* make you well. (But on June 14, 1994, "Doctors warn that prayer without treatment can be deadly"—no Christian Science here.) Science (or at least reputable authority) attests to wonders, which in turn attest to the truths of faith. Nothing is ever debunked, although occasionally unnamed skeptics are trotted out as foils. When a photograph displayed Jesus' face hovering over "war-torn Somalia," the *News* reported on March 2, 1993 that "skeptics were quick to argue that the face was nothing more than a meaningless illusion created by an ordinary storm. But no less a figure than Pope John Paul II believes that the face was a sign from God with implications for every man, woman and child on the planet." To the tabloids, science and religion combine to confound the skeptics; there is but a single kind of truth.

From the burning bush to the Pentecost, Jewish and Christian Scriptures show a Deity that makes itself known by the tangible evidence of signs and wonders. The tabloids try to do no less. That is not to say they are innocent of fabricating stories and doctoring photographs. Defending itself in 1991 against a libel suit from an Arkansas nonagenarian whom it reported to be pregnant, the *Sun* argued that it wasn't a newspaper, that it made most of its stories up, and that it was therefore exempt from journalistic standards. According to the *Sun*'s lawyer, Phillip Anderson, "Most reasonable people recognize that the stories are essentially fiction."[3] This characterization does not appear to apply to regular tabloid readers, who, Bird found, believe some stories, disbelieve others, and would like to believe still others. Bird concludes that such readers, who number in the millions, allow tabloids to "reinforce their already existing beliefs while finding no inconsistency in dismissing stories about subjects they did not have faith in."[4]

Whether or not most tabloid readers are, by the *Sun*'s self-serving standard, reasonable people, there can be no question that the miracle stories reinforce their religious beliefs. Most Americans believe in the existence of God and the devil, the accuracy of the Bible, and the efficacy of prayer.[5] In more subtle ways as well, tabloid spirituality is tied into the culture at large. The *Weekly World News*'s photograph of the woman's soul rising from an operating table, for example, is a classic spiritualist rendering of soul and body—a direct iconographic descendent of a deathbed scene pictured in the autobiography of the nineteenth-century American clairvoyant Andrew Jackson Davis.[6] A November 1, 1988, *News* story reporting the weight of the human soul at $\frac{1}{3,000}$ th of an ounce reflects (in the view of the historian Caroline Walker Bynum) wide-ranging concerns about material continuity and body integrity in late-twentieth-century American society.[7]

So is it the reputable news organizations that are out of touch with the public mind? Do they shun reporting supernatural phenomena, and, if so, is it because the phenomena fail to meet standards of empirical proof or because the journalists inhabit a culture of disbelief? These are not simple questions to answer. But it seems clear that, whatever journalists' personal beliefs, the mainstream news media's approach to the supernatural has become more tabloid than skeptical—often less skeptical than that of church authorities.

The reason is that the prevailing topos has to do not with the truth or falsity of the phenomenon in question, but with the faith of those who believe. Perhaps the purest mainstream exponent of this topos of supernatural belief or good faith can be found in *Life* magazine since its reincarnation as a supermarket commodity. *Life*'s March 1994 cover story, "The Power of Prayer," is almost unmediated vox populi: a succession of statements by different Americans explaining why they pray, accompanied by survey data about Americans' praying habits. A brief introduction states that "humankind is praying in astonishing numbers," that "spiritual fervor is shimmering in the U.S.," and that nine out of ten Americans, "ignoring speculation that God is dead, pray frequently and earnestly—and almost all say God has answered their prayers."[8]

Such remarks are expressions of a spiritual populism that exalts the faith of the humble over elitist unbelief. In its July 1991 issue on miracles, *Life* assumed this philosophical posture by way of a thumbnail history of religion in America. The villain of the piece was the rationalistic deism of the Founding Fathers, which allowed no place for the miraculous. Thus was created, said *Life*, a public culture in which government, the schools, and "eventually the mass media" became enemies of strong expressions of faith— "reality police" (according to Boston University sociologist Peter Berger) for whom miracles were out of bounds. But the "catch" was that "almost everybody outside the deists' immediate circle was content to lead a life of reality crime." In the nineteenth century, great numbers of American Christians abandoned tame mainline churches for those that sought out the miraculous. Then there were the millions of immigrants "with faith unpolluted by rationalist doubts." And so there developed "a contradiction between official skepticism and popular belief."[9] *Life*, of course, was on the side of the people.

The issue featured a long, moving article by contributing editor Tom Junod about one severely ill woman's pilgrimage to Medjugorje, the Croatian village where the Virgin Mary had been appearing for a decade to several young people. This was in keeping with the magazine's passion for stories of "suffering, with moral uplift," Junod recalled in February 1993. "The tabs' influence on *Life* was beyond enormous, and the miracle story was of a piece with that." His own interest had been to "capture the experience, the sensation, of religious faith." He had accompanied Carol Leland, a thirty-seven-year-old Albuquerque woman, on her search not so much for healing as for a sign of the divine presence. In Medjugorje, she received her sign, but nearly died from lack of oxygen at the high altitude: "Outside her window pilgrims were praying for her, hoping for a miracle, but Carol's own miracle had occurred long ago. She had never despaired of God. She had never lost faith, and later there were some pilgrims who said that it was not Medjugorje but rather Carol's faith in life and in God that had restored their own."[10] Did Carol Leland actually see the blue light she claimed to see? Did something truly supernatural happen on her journey of faith? "The ending was crafted to be completely ambiguous," Junod said. "The whole point of the story was private miracles. If you have a woman like Carol who is claiming a subjective experience and telling you about it, who am I to say that that experience didn't happen?"

In the wake of Medjugorje, a host of Marian apparitions began to be reported around the world, a trend that itself became news.[11] Although rarely handled with as much skill as Junod's story, first-time or one-shot feature stories on an apparition generally hewed to the topos of the pilgrims' faith, whether their destination was a natural spring in the Bronx or a farm in north Georgia.[12] To be sure, if the phenomenon was such that it drew regular coverage, other angles and topoi had to be sought out. Such was the case with the Marian apparition in the Atlanta exurb of Conyers.

There, in October 1990, a middle-aged homemaker named Nancy Fowler began claiming that on the thirteenth of every month she received messages for the United States from the Virgin Mary. As word of the messages got out, pilgrims began to turn up at her home. Before long, a wealthy supporter bought Fowler a nearby farm, where attendance reached an apparent peak of about seventy thousand on November 13, 1993. On "apparition day," the pilgrims, many of them Hispanics from southern Florida, would gather on folding chairs and blankets around the farmhouse. At noon, members of Fowler's volunteer organization, Our Loving Mother's Children, would begin to lead the assemblage in praying the Rosary while Fowler waited in the "apparition room" for her visitation. After an hour or so of prayer, it would be announced that Mary had arrived, and as Fowler received her words they would be immediately transmitted in English and Spanish to those outside. Here and there, meanwhile, pilgrims would report smelling roses, seeing the sun spinning, and detecting other signs of Mary's presence. Some would point Polaroid cameras at the sun, and sometimes the photo would show an oblong space with a gleam of light in the middle, an image taken to represent the door of heaven. After Mary's departure, Fowler would come out on the farmhouse porch, read the message again, and offer her own thoughts. By then, the pilgrims would already have started drifting back to their cars and tour buses.

The *Atlanta Journal-Constitution* published its first article on the apparition on September 14, 1991. Religion writer Gayle White set the scene of the faithful staring into the midday sun, "oohing, sobbing and praising the Lord." The story told of Fowler's background and claims and made reference to other Marian apparitions. White followed this up the next week with a lengthy overview of the apparition trend. As month followed month, the Fowler story became the responsibility of the reporter assigned to cover Rockdale County. The rate of recurrence made it ideal for regular coverage; between the first article and June 1994 (when the messages to America, although not the visitations, purportedly ceased), the newspaper published some fifty stories on the apparition, ranging in length from briefs to extended takeouts. The number of pilgrims was tracked, as was the traffic problem, the county commission's efforts at regulating the monthly influx, and the pilgrims' impact on the local economy. When someone set fire to several of the portable toilets scattered around the farm, that too was duly noted.

For more than a year, the Rockdale beat reporter was Bill Osinski, who brought a clearly skeptical edge to the story. For instance, in his April 14 report on that month's apparition he noted dryly, "Aside from the glories of a full-bloom spring day in the country, there were no miraculous signs of the supernatural that all could see." Then, on June 13, Osinski wrote a lengthy story focusing on three disillusioned former associates of Fowler. According to them, the Conyers visionary was subject to erratic mood swings; sometimes expressed the desire to be a nun even though she was married; and prepared some of the monthly messages in advance from apparitions she supposedly witnessed a day or two earlier. The story noted that the associates had been hesitant to discuss the private life of a woman "whom so many people have placed their faith in." In line with the topos of supernatural belief, the headline read: "Three of Little Faith."

"We have a responsibility to depict the truth of what's happening out there," Osinski said in June 1994. "I think we tend to take things at face value." But the story had effectively ended his ability to report on Fowler. "I had to rule myself out, because in my coverage I had become very opinionated," he said. In his view, the newspaper as a whole should have withdrawn from reporting on the apparition. "I am concerned that subsequent stories have played it straight, and given [Fowler] and her followers more credit than they deserve." His own reaction to the proceedings had never been positive. "I happen to be Catholic myself. I think it's kind of embarrassing." Yet he had not been "trying to disparage" the pilgrims' faith. "It's a tricky question because you never want to be disrespectful of someone's belief. The people who come are generally sincere. It is a spiritual experience. The question I've had is about the woman at the center of all this."

In fact, his exposé was crafted to include the side of true belief. Its final paragraphs told about a former Richmond, Virginia, television journalist and talk-show host who had become one of Fowler's devotees. There was also a sidebar on the Virginia businessman whose experience of the apparitions led him to purchase the farm and otherwise support Fowler (and who was, Osinski decided, a sincere believer and not a profiteer). All in all, those inclined to think Fowler a charlatan or a mental case had some evidence before them, but the believers were also given testimonials to support their faith.

Such balance, or ambiguity, is characteristic of stories that raise the possibility of religious fraud in allegedly supernatural events. *U.S. News and World Report*, for example, devoted its March 29, 1993 (Easter) cover story to investigating reports of a Pittsburgh priest in whose presence statues of the Madonna supposedly wept. "Is it a miracle or hoax?" the magazine asked and went on to explore the ways a weeping-statue hoax could be carried off. The story nonetheless concluded on an agnostic note, declaring that "until the Lord takes to skywriting his message," the reality of such phenomena was likely to remain unsettled. "Which leaves us, in the end, with just a priest, some statues and a host of decent people, dreaming a beautiful dream. Whether the dream is real, and what it means, are up to you to decide."[13]

The newsweeklies display a particular weakness for this kind of saccharine spirituality. Consider the final paragraph of *Time*'s Christmas 1993 cover story on angels:

> The act of looking for angels is an exalting gesture. To the degree that this search represents the triumph of hope over proof, it may be a good and cheering sign of our time. For all those who say they have had some direct experience of angels, no proof is necessary; for those predisposed to doubt angels' existence, no proof is possible. And for those in the mystified middle there is often a growing desire to be persuaded. If heaven is willing to sing to us, it is little to ask that we be ready to listen.[14]

What is exalting about looking for angels? Why is no proof possible for those predisposed to doubt? Churlish to ask. It's Christmastime and it's a wonderful life.

If nothing else, the sentimental celebration of popular belief insulates the news media from charges of impiety. But even better protection is provided by the Catholic church, which is famously reluctant to place its imprimatur on the miraculous. The papacy has been in the business of authenticating miracles since it took control of the process of canonizing saints in 1234. Since then, too, the church has been well aware of the difficulty of knowing whether a real miracle has taken place. Aquinas argued that although witnesses might give false testimony, it was "piously to be believed" that the judgment of the church could not err.[15] Some of the greatest canon lawyers of the Middle Ages went further, holding that the church could err and that the pope himself could not, on the basis of external evidence, know for certain that a miraculous event had taken place.[16]

It is thus appropriate that a standard tabloid argument for the authenticity of a miracle is: "Even the Vatican agrees." Most of the time, the local Catholic bishop will remain aloof from an apparition; on occasion he will investigate its authenticity, find no evidence of supernatural origin, and order the faithful to stay away.[17] In the Conyers story, the *Journal-Constitution* regularly noted the efforts of Atlanta archbishop James Lyke to discourage attendance at the Fowler farm. After Lyke's death in 1993, the new archbishop, John F. Donoghue, was quoted as saying that, although he did not know whether Mary was appearing there, he had seen evidence that the apparition had inspired some to return to the church, others to convert—a sign of archiepiscopal favor that Fowler's supporters received with great pleasure.

Some find ill-advised the church's interest in distinguishing real miracles from those explicable in natural or psychological or fraudulent terms. In her well-received book on the cult of the Virgin, Marina Warner points out that what was considered "holy fire" in the Middle Ages is now understood by medical science to be ergotism, a disease contracted by eating fungus-infected rye.

By insisting that the supernatural is only manifest in the unnatural, the Church renders itself extremely vulnerable to scientific discovery, which can make its decisions look foolish. It could instead adopt the position of absolute faith and maintain that as God is everywhere, his miraculous work informs all natural phenomena—including cures, both startling and otherwise. Miracles would then increase a hundredfold. This would correspond to the conviction of most Catholics, who are men of great faith (most pilgrims to Lourdes see a miracle cure while they are there). It would also put an end to the lip-service that scientific bodies like the Medical Records Office at Lourdes pay to nineteenth-century rationalism as they attempt the impossible task of reconciling the religious and scientific systems of thought.[18]

But absolute faith is not what people tend to have, and the effort to disengage the supernatural from the natural, impossible though it may be, remains a matter of enduring interest. When CBS-TV's "48 Hours" visited the Vatican on December 15, 1988, it spent a good deal of time with the medical office charged with examining whether a given healing event is beyond the ability of science to explain and therefore due to supernatural causes. The importance of miracles to the general populace is fully grasped by the *Sun,* which on November 10, 1992, featured a photograph of the Virgin Mary accompanying Pope John Paul II on an airplane flight. Vatican officials, said the paper, "see the possibility of a proven miracle as a way to strengthen spirituality around the world." As one "insider" put it, "This is a reward for all those men and women who've had doubts about God in their lives. The pictures of the Virgin Mary gives [*sic*] us support from the highest authority in the universe."

It could, of course, be argued that the news media's readiness to accept the testimony of believers stems from no more than an institutional bar against giving offense. Yet a willingness to lend some credence to events apparently inexplicable in scientific terms is not confined to matters of popular religious faith. In a study of 222 psychic phenomena stories that appeared in the *Cleveland Plain Dealer,* the *Columbus Dispatch,* the *New York Times,* and the *Washington Post* between 1977 and 1988, Roger Klare found that uncritical or credulous stories outnumbered skeptical ones 46 percent to 17 percent, with the balance neutral or indeterminate.[19] Do journalists believe in ghosts, psychokinesis, and ESP? It doesn't matter. Psychic events are entertaining, and debunking them takes a lot more work than simply reporting the accounts of those who claim to have experienced them. Moreover, as Philip Meyer notes in the *Columbia Journalism Review,* "The human desire to believe is so strong and the stories are so intrinsically interesting that the temptation to suspend critical judgment is almost irresistible." [20]

If journalists covering the supernatural willingly suspend their disbelief, that is not to say that the resulting stories are identical to those that appear in specifically religious publications. In the Middle Ages, miracle stories served a host of doctrinal purposes; the tales of demoniacs who know hidden sins (chapter 1), for example, were used to encourage lay people to go to confession. Similarly, accounts of Marian apparitions in apparitionist publications promote doctrines, devotions, and warnings about a heavenly chastisement to come.[21] Charismatic Protestant accounts of healing miracles tend to focus on the conversion experience of the person healed—as witness the cover of *Charisma and Christian Life*'s special miracles issue in November 1991: "A crippling disease put this Jewish woman in a wheelchair . . . until she found her Messiah and Healer." Such publications are not at all interested in the kind of studied ambiguity that characterizes some of the best of the news media's coverage.

Nothing better illustrates the contrast in approach than two movies about the Rapture, the premillennialist doctrine that those who are saved will be snatched into heaven before the "tribulation" that is supposed to precede Christ's second coming. *The Thief in the Night*, made in 1972 by evangelical film maker Donald W. Thompson, is a doctrinally correct sermon about a young woman who cannot commit her life to Christ. After the Rapture steals away her believing friends, she is left to fend for herself in a nightmarish world of fascistic anti-Christians. By contrast, Michael Tolkin's film *The Rapture* (1991) is a psychological study of religious conversion gone wrong. After living a life of flagrant sin, a young woman joins an evangelical group and begins to lead an exemplary life. When a madman kills her husband, she takes her daughter into the desert in the expectation that they will both be snatched bodily into heaven. When this doesn't happen, she despairingly shoots the girl to death and is put in jail. But then the tribulation actually arrives, and she is given the opportunity to enter heaven. She declines, unable to forgive God for her misery on earth.

The Rapture played to decidedly mixed reviews in both the religious and general press. In *Christian Century* on October 23, 1991, Marilynne S. Mason called it "slick, calculating and manipulative." Michael Medved saw the film's Christian believers as "twitching zombies" and claimed its message was unequivocally antireligious.[22] But Ted Baehr, the evangelical who heads the national Christian Film and Television Commission, compared *The Rapture* favorably to *The Thief*

in the Night and others of its ilk. Reviewing the film in his Christian movie guide, he contended that it was "not heretical, nor does
it mock Christians," and called it "an intelligent call to make a decision about the ultimate meaning of life."[23] Baehr has remarked that
just as communist films are boring because they were made to please
party bosses, so "Christian films are boring because you make them
to please the church party bosses."[24] Freedom from church bosses and
the need to address a wide audience can result in journalism and art
that offers a more profound image of religion than orthodoxy may
supply. It's worth recalling that, from an orthodox Christian point of
view, both Dante and Milton leave something to be desired.

Yet for true believers, subtlety and spiritual profundity are likely
to matter less than communicating the truth that sets people free. An
article in *Notre Dame Magazine* on media coverage of the Conyers
apparition posed the question in large type: "Journalists are trained to
stay outside a story. But what if it might be the story of the century?"
The author, Darrell Laurent of the *Lynchburg* [Va.] *News and Advance*,
actually had little specific to criticize in the news media's coverage of
Nancy Fowler. Instead, he focused on the way such religion stories
seem to threaten the journalist's "objective 'comfort zone.'" He himself saw no spinning suns or dancing rose petals on his two trips to
Conyers, but he plainly wished he had.[25]

One might ask, If a journalist actually witnessed a supernatural
phenomenon, would he or she be able to report it? In Conyers on
May 13, 1994, a WSB-Radio reporter named Paula Lin, disparaging
the scene of prayers and Polaroids, said, "But I'm bummed, anyway.
I was hoping to see something." Tom Junod, thinking back to his
trip to Medjugorje, recalled that at the time his wife had been having
health problems. "I would not have been averse to a miracle. You get
plunged into their context of belief as a sophisticated observer, yet
even sophisticated observers are not above wishing for miracles. But I
didn't really buy it."

The problem, Laurent suggested, is that supernatural phenomena
tease journalists with the promise of hard evidence. His remedy, however, was anything but radical: "Just be reporters. Talk to people and
report what they say. Report what you see. Don't make judgments,
but don't ignore it."[26] It is exactly what most of them do.

NOTES

1. John Siegenthaler, "Introduction," in John Dart and Jimmy Allen, *Bridging the Gap: Religion and the News Media* (Nashville: Freedom Forum First Amendment Center, 1993), 3.

2. S. Elizabeth Bird, *For Enquiring Minds: A Cultural Study of Supermarket Tabloids* (Knoxville: University of Tennessee Press, 1992), 201.

3. Associated Press, December 3, 1991. In 1993, the U.S. Supreme Court let stand the jury's verdict and the woman, then ninety-eight, received $1 million in damages (*Chicago Tribune*, October 20, 1993).

4. Bird, *For Enquiring Minds*, 121.

5. For a lighthearted account of God and the afterlife according to the tabloids, see Daniel McDonald, "God's Favorite Number," *Christian Century*, December 12, 1990, 1158–59.

6. Andrew Jackson Davis, *The Magic Staff: An Autobiography* (New York: J. S. Brown), 1859. I am grateful to Catherine Albanese for calling my attention to this parallel.

7. Caroline Walker Bynum, *Fragmentation and Redemption: Essays on Gender and the Human Body in Medieval Religion* (New York: Zone Books, 1991), 250.

8. *Life* (March 1994): 54.

9. *Life* (July 1991): 38–39.

10. Ibid., 36.

11. For example, "Apparitions Sweeping the United States," Associated Press, May 21, 1993.

12. On the "Lourdes of the Bronx," a shrine at Saint Lucy's Roman Catholic Church, see the *New York Times*, May 27, 1992. For the story of a pilgrimage to Conyers comparable to Junod's *Life* article, see the *Philadelphia Inquirer*, February 16, 1994.

13. *U.S. News and World Report*, March 29, 1993, 55.

14. *Time*, December 27, 1993, 65.

15. Thomas Aquinas, *Quodlibetum IX*, art. xvi; *Opera omnia IX* (Parma, 1859), 599.

16. For example, see Innocent IV, *In quinque decretalia libros commentaria* (Venice, 1570), 271; Henry of Susa, *In tertium decretalium librum commentaria* (Venice, 1581), 172; Augustine of Ancona, *Summa de potestate ecclesiastica* (Rome, 1479), Quaestio XIV, art. 4. For a discussion of these texts, and of the development of this skeptical view within the church, see Mark Silk, "*Scientia rerum:* The Place of Example in Later Medieval Thought," unpublished Ph.D. diss., Harvard University, 1982, ch. 10.

17. That was the response of Denver Archbishop J. Francis Stafford to reported appearances of the Virgin Mary to a thirty-two-year-old woman at

the Mother Cabrini shrine twenty miles from downtown Denver. Religious News Service, May 12, 1993; March 9, 1994.

18. Marina Warner, *Alone of All Her Sex: The Myth and the Cult of the Virgin Mary* (New York: Vintage Books, 1983), 310.

19. Roger Klare, "Ghosts Make News," *Skeptical Inquirer* 14 (Summer 1990): 363–71.

20. Philip Meyer, "Ghostbooster: The Press and the Paranormal," *Columbia Journalism Review* 25 (March-April 1986): 39. For opposite approaches taken by the Milwaukee newspapers to a haunted-house story, see Barrett J. Brunsman, "Ghost Story," *The Quill* 76 (April 1988): 25–30. For an argument in favor of more skeptical coverage, see Kendrick Frazier, "How to Cover 'Psychics' and the Paranormal," *Bulletin of the American Society of Newspaper Editors* (April 1982): 16–19.

21. See, for instance, *Our Lady Queen of Peace,* published by the Pittsburgh Center for Peace, or *Signs of the Times,* a glossy magazine published by Agnus Dei Publications in Sterling, Virginia.

22. Michael Medved, *Hollywood vs. America: Popular Culture and the War on Traditional Values* (New York: HarperCollins Publishers, 1992), 58.

23. Review by Bruce Williams and Ted Baehr in *Movieguide,* October 25, 1991, 9.

24. Terry Mattingly, "Why Christian Films Are Boring," Religious News Service, May 2, 1993.

25. Darrell Laurent, "The Limits of Objectivity," *Notre Dame Magazine* (Winter 1993–94): 23.

26. Laurent, "The Limits of Objectivity," 27.

CHAPTER ELEVEN

Declension

And ye have done worse than your fathers; for, be-
hold, ye walk every one after the imagination of his
evil heart, that they may not hearken unto me.

JEREMIAH 16:12

If *Life* magazine's miracles issue was an expression of spiritual populism, it also told a tale of endemic institutional decline. Since the
founding of the country, according to *Life*, it's been one religious
upheaval after another, "as great numbers of American Christians
deemed the dominant faiths of their periods too tame, too bureaucra-
tized, too unconcerned with God's day-to-day involvement in human
affairs."[1] There is something to be said for this outline of American
religious history. Would it have been limned in the years after World
War II, when the Protestant establishment was riding high?

In a decade-by-decade survey of religion coverage in *Time* and
Newsweek from the 1930s through the 1980s, Dennis Voskuil found
that, until the early 1960s, nearly half was related either directly or
indirectly to one of the mainline Protestant denominations.[2] *Time,*
whose presiding genius was a Presbyterian missionary's son, put just
about every prominent American Protestant leader you could think
of on its cover between World War II and 1961. Within Protestantism,
a disproportionate amount of attention was paid to that most establishmentarian of all denominations, the Episcopal church. A study of
coverage of nine Protestant denominations in *Time, Newsweek,* the
New York Times, the *Washington Post,* and two small Pennsylvania
dailies in 1974 shows nearly three times more stories about Episcopa-
lians than about the second-ranking Lutherans.[3]

But coverage of mainline Protestantism dropped off sharply after the Eisenhower revival had run its course. In the 1970s, the Catholic church began to get more ink in *Time* and *Newsweek* than mainline Protestantism, and there was a sharp rise in the coverage of fundamentalists, Pentecostals, and other Protestant outsiders. By the 1980s, the media had become well aware, thanks to the efforts of various sociologists of American religion, that the mainline was in numerical decline. In 1989, *Time* sounded the valedictory. "In the beginning was mainline Protestantism," it began. And the mainline was with America, and the mainline was America:

> At Plymouth Rock and Jamestown, and for 3½ centuries thereafter, the denominations known today by that label defined the spiritual and moral ethos of the U.S. These prominent WASP bastions nurtured the founders, imparting to them notions of republican government and individual freedom. Dominating American Protestantism, these churches shaped virtually every aspect of an evolving nation: its pioneering colleges, its nineteenth century novels of sin and rectitude, its capitalist ethic of striving and saving, and a world-conquering spirit that was shared by missionaries and entrepreneurs alike. Mainliners were at the forefront of social crusades from independence to abolition, women's suffrage to Prohibition, civil rights to Viet Nam protests.

But during the past two decades, "that center has dropped away." An unprecedented decline in membership had left mainline Protestantism in "deep trouble." The explanation? Religion writer Richard Ostling offered several, but they all boiled down to spiritual fecklessness: "low-cal theology," "wishy-washy liberalism," and an habitual inclination to sit back on its haunches and wait for new membership to walk in the door.[4]

This is hardly the place to evaluate the merits of such an assessment. The point to note is that the decline in media attention to the mainline precedes the awareness — and even the reality — of the mainline's numerical decline. Indeed, the explanation for the decline precedes the decline in attention. One need look no farther than *Life*'s report on "third force" Christianity, defined by the president of New York's Union Seminary, Henry P. Van Dusen, as comprising Pentecostal, Adventist, and other churches that emphasize direct experience of the Holy Spirit. Calling the third force "the most extraordinary religious phenomenon of our time," Van Dusen wrote: "Its groups preach a direct biblical message readily understood. They commonly promise an immediate, life-transforming experience of the living-God-in-Christ which is far more significant to many individuals than the version of it normally found in conventional churches. They directly approach people—in their homes, on the streets, anywhere—and do not wait for them to come to church."[5] In 1958, of course, the "conventional churches" were thriving, at least as far as the numbers went. But their problem was the same. It had always been the same. Since the days of the Puritans, American religious leaders have rarely let slip the opportunity to lament the decline of religious devotion. Since the Great Awakening, America's conventional churches have always seemed to be falling asleep. Nor is this topos of declension shunned by today's news media.

But the cure sometimes seems worse than the disease. The media are wedded to the values of tolerance and inclusion that the conventional churches preach. They also show a certain fondness for the traditional role of such churches—their dignified serving up of time-honored spiritual goods, their nonconfrontational style, their central location in the larger community, and their mildly constraining attitude toward the surrounding commercial culture. Is religion not a refuge from the getting and striving of the workaday world? To note, as Ostling did, that the mainline churches "are sorely lacking in the marketing and communications savvy that the Evangelicals employ to win new members," was not the same as unambivalently applauding the use of such techniques.[6]

From May 18–21, 1993, Gary Trudeau devoted his Doonesbury comic strip to market-driven religion. The strip's eponymous hero, Michael Doonesbury, returns to the site of his college commune and finds that it has been transformed into a church by the perfectly liberal Reverend Sloan. The Rev. has tired of trying to corral uninterested undergraduates into the campus chapel. He tells Mike how he began with a focus group to gauge peoples' needs, then instituted aerobics, yoga, and bingo, twelve-step recovery programs, a soup kitchen, and cooking classes. "Members are far more consumer conscious than they used to be," he explains. In the final strip, Mike asks about God. While granting that God has still got the "big name," the minister allows as how it isn't invoked very often: "Um, frankly, Mike, God comes with a lot of baggage. The whole male, Eurocentric guilt thing."

This is plainly a satire on Willow Creek Community Church in South Barrington, Illinois, the megachurch that began with a door-to-door survey to find out what people wanted in the way of an ecclesiastical institution.[7] Displaying none of the symbolic trappings of Christianity, Willow Creek is known for its multimedia "seekers" services, which by steering clear of explicit Christian doctrine invite congregants to worship in the least threatening way possible. The church also pioneered the kinds of personal support groups that have become a standard feature of large churches around the country. But in contrast to Reverend Sloan's politically correct college-town theology, Willow Creek is anything but godless. Inspired by the ideas of a biblical studies professor at Wheaton College (Billy Graham's alma mater), it represents another in the long history of American evangelical efforts to reach out to the unchurched masses. Alongside the seekers at Willow Creek are an equal number of those who have found the Way—who take communion, sing traditional hymns a cappella, and acknowledge Jesus as their personal lord and savior.

A 1989 story in *Time* contrasted Willow Creek's multimedia appeal with "the stodgy ritual and sanctimoniousness of many traditional churches."[8] An article in *Woman's Day* praised Willow Creek for being spiritually up-to-date: "There is no fire-and-brimstone here. No Bible-thumping. Just practical, witty messages designed to hit the listeners where they live."[9] Grabbing the other end of the elephant, Michael Hirsley of the *Chicago Tribune* emphasized on May 21, 1989 that behind the soft sell lay an unvarnished version of the old-time religion.

Yet there is also a sense that the wide gate and broad ways of megachurches like Willow Creek make religion too easy. In a tart *Wall Street Journal* story on Houston's Second Baptist Church, R. Gustav Niebuhr pointed out that the church "does as much marketing as proselytizing" (a slightly murky distinction). While noting that "for some, the spiritual life is still the main attraction," Niebuhr focused on the convenient parking and spotless day-care facilities, the rock concerts and wrestling matches, all calculated to put customers in the church's plush seats. Not that the church deserved all the blame for this outpouring of creature comforts, however; it had been driven to it by the unregenerate state of the baby boom generation. "Like most megachurches, it is primarily designed for a generation unversed in theology, essentially nonsectarian and unsentimental about the old neighborhood church." As for the religion itself: "The Christianity they do serve up is mostly conservative and to-the-point, stripped of most of the old hymns, liturgy and denominational dogma that tend to bore the video gen- eration."[10] There is something wrong, somehow, with a church that gives folks what they want instead of what they need.

This critique recalls the rough treatment that Niebuhr's great-uncle Reinhold meted out to Billy Graham's ministry in a famous *Life* maga- zine article in 1957: "It would be interesting to know how many of those attracted by his evangelistic Christianity are attracted by the obvious fact that his new evangelism is much blander than the old. For it promises a new life, not through painful religious experience but merely by signing a decision card. Thus a miracle of regeneration is promised at a painless price by an obviously sincere evangelist. It is a bargain."[11] A distrust of mass religious appeal has been a staple of American high culture since George Whitefield began leading open- air revivals in the late 1730s. During the Great Awakening, the per- ceived danger was enthusiasm. In the 1990s, the critique has tended to focus on religious consumerism and a kind of spiritual footlooseness.

In its angels issue, *Time* worried that contemporary belief had the markings of a take-it-or-leave-it New Age cult: "Only in the New Age would it be possible to invent an angel so mellow that it can be ignored."[12] A few months earlier—in *Time*'s Easter 1993 cover story, "The Generation That Forgot God"—Ostling contrasted the good old days of strong, traditional faith with the helter-skelter present.

> There was a time in America when a spiritual journey meant
> a long, stormy crossing of the soul, an exploration mapped by
> Scripture and led by clergy through the family church. Catholic
> you were born and Catholic you died, or Methodist, or Jew. . . .
> Today, a quiet revolution is taking place. . . . Increasing numbers
> of baby boomers who left the fold years ago are turning religious
> again, but many are traveling from church to church or faith to
> faith, sampling creeds, shopping for a custom-made God.

Ostling might have mentioned that the boomers were just cutting their spiritual teeth when *Time* asked, on its Easter 1966 cover, "Is God Dead?" Small wonder they had to fend for themselves. He did acknowledge that there was "genuine creativity" in the "reconfigured faiths" and that "much is gained" when houses of worship address "real needs" rather than purveying "old abstractions, expectations, and mannerisms." But the bottom line was cautionary. "Many of those who have rediscovered churchgoing may ultimately be shortchanged, however, if the focus of their faith seems subtly to shift from the glorification of God to the gratification of man."[13]

In a four-part series on West Coast religious experimentation, the *San Francisco Chronicle*'s religion editor, Don Lattin, struck a similar balance: "This spiritual openness, this religious individualism, is a blessing and a curse. It gives people great freedom to explore their soul and psyche, to find their own spiritual path, but it can also leave them lost and lonely, exploited and spiritually manipulated by sinister cults and paranoid prophets."[14]

Religion in America is characterized by nothing if not persistent experimentation and, as *Life* suggested, a succession of shifts of spiritual allegiance. The news media reflect, in not always coherent ways, all the confusing religious mythology at large in the society: that the old-time religion is in trouble; that the peoples' faith is strong; that the big brick church on the public square is the place to worship; and that the real spiritual action is on the margins. And, just as the existing religious establishments are always doomed to decline, just as the latest generation always seems worse than the one before, so there is always the hope, the promise, the necessity of a religious revival just around the corner.

NOTES

1. *Life* (July 1991): 39.
2. Dennis Voskuil, "Reaching Out: Protestantism and the Media," in *Between the Times: The Travail of the Protestant Establishment in America, 1900–1960*, ed. William Hutchison (Cambridge: Cambridge University Press, 1989), 78–80.
3. Douglas Spencer Campbell, "News of Religion in the Secular Press," master's thesis, Pennsylvania State University, 1976, 121.
4. *Time*, May 22, 1989, 94–96. A similar if less portentous review of the decline of the mainline can be found in the *Atlanta Journal-Constitution*, November 26, 1992.
5. *Life*, June 9, 1958, 123.
6. *Time*, May 22, 1989, 94.
7. In fact, not only conservative evangelical churches have been influenced

by the Willow Creek model. In 1992 the liberal Evangelical Lutheran church decided to establish several Willow Creek-style megachurches in California. See *Atlanta Journal-Constitution,* April 18, 1992.

8. *Time,* March 16, 1989, 60.

9. *Women's Day* did detect a couple of flies in the ointment: impersonality in a church that attracts as many as fifteen thousand worshipers every weekend, and "some resistance" for its multi-million-dollar operating budget — "because of the needs of the poor throughout the world." Susan Headden, "Worshiping God Big Time," *Women's Day,* October 13, 1992, 114 (5).

10. R. Gustav Niebuhr, "Megachurches Strive to Be All Things to All Parishioners," *Wall Street Journal,* May 13, 1991.

11. *Life,* July 1, 1957, 92.

12. *Time,* December 27, 1993, 56.

13. *Time,* April 5, 1993, 44.

14. Religious News Service, June 28, 1993.

CHAPTER TWELVE

Unsecular
Media

———

After a United Airlines plane crashed in Iowa in the summer of 1989, the president of the Freedom From Religion Foundation, a Wisconsin-based atheists' organization, sent a letter to the managing editors of the nation's news services deploring the prevalence of what she called "bible-belt journalism." Despite the deaths of more than a hundred people, Anne Gaylor complained, all across the country there were headlines that read "God Opened a Hole for Escape" and "God Looks Out for Jet Passengers": "What we have in the United States today is an army of gullible news people. Why does no one ever ask, when these superstitious claims are publicized, why 'God' let the tragedies occur in the first place? What century are we living in? Why didn't their omnipotent 'God' just fix the hydraulic system of United Flight 232 and save everybody!" Gaylor urged that the AP style book be revised to warn journalists against giving God the credit, never the blame; reporting miracles or other unsubstantiated paranormal events; seeking out only religionists for comment on disasters, deaths, or incredible tales; and presenting story after story on the efficacy of prayer. In a word, she wanted reporters and editors to abandon their "cheerleading role" when it came to religion.[1]

Militant atheists are not much of a constituency in twentieth-century America, and it is doubtful whether any of the managing editors gave more than a moment's thought to Gaylor's plea. But as strangers in a strange land, atheists see religion embedded in the culture where most of us don't notice it at all. They are not just seeing things.

In the preceding chapters I have tried to show that the news media, far from promoting a secularist agenda of their own, approach religion with values and presuppositions that the American public widely shares. Certainly, compared to the vitriol and satire of Franklin's *Courant* or Bennett's *Herald* or Mencken's *Sun,* such criticism of religion as appears in today's news media is thin gruel indeed. William Randolph Hearst, who knew how to turn news into money, once said, "Newspapers do not form the opinion of the public; but if they are to be successful, they must express the opinion of the public."[2] Today's news executives are not less interested in commercial success; newspapers in particular, preoccupied with their declining market share, are at great pains to give readers a product that meets their needs and sensibilities. Hostility to religion is hardly the order of the day.

But if that is the case, why do so many religious people appear to believe otherwise?

In part, it is because people fail to register what gives no offense. From reports on good works to exposés of "cults," a lot of religion news does not strike most consumers of news as reflecting any point of view, precisely because it is a point of view they share. The few religion scholars and civil libertarians who object to hostile news coverage of unconventional religious groups are voices crying in the wilderness.

At the same time, the most important news from the religion front over the past two decades has been turbulent and contentious. Domestically, religious groups have campaigned against the social legitimation of abortion, homosexuality, and other transgressions against what they believe to be traditional family values. Abroad, too, religion has seemed to be on the march. The main story line for the end of the twentieth century is that people of faith are leading a counterrevolution against a morally impaired, if not bankrupt, secular society—of which the mass media are the most familiar expression. What has escaped notice is that the media have told this story largely from the standpoint of the religious themselves.

Although the Western press had been unconvinced that the Shah of Iran was the modernizing leader he claimed to be, after the Shiite revolution reporters swallowed the Ayatollah Khomeini's Manichaean view of Islam versus modernity whole—and used it as the explanation for just about anything that happened in the Muslim world.[3] Journalists also bought into the claim of the ayatollah and other Muslim militants that they were restoring an ancient pattern of theocratic governance, even though historians of Islam could readily have told them that this Islamicist model of the state was something new under the Muslim sun.

After 1980, when the Christian Right burst onto the American political scene, what had been referred to as "militant Islam" now became "Islamic fundamentalism" — as if Shiite mullahs and Southern Baptist preachers shared approximately the same worldview. In a striking example of this religious amalgam, the 1992 PBS series "Fundamentalisms Observed" discerned one overarching reality in a heterogeneous collection of actively religious people in Israel, the Arab world, and the United States: "For these men, and thousands like them, religion is providing an identity and a purpose for life. They are fighting back, against their own sins, and the sins of society. They are called fundamentalists. This is their story."

In the wake of the bombing of the World Trade Center, *Time* offered some justification for the "militant fundamentalist anger" of Muslims: "The West and some of what comes with it (AIDS, drugs, pornography, the destruction of family and community, for example) are in many ways as dangerous and repulsive as a fundamentalist Muslim may believe."[4] In its 1993 series on American Muslims, the *New York Times* raised the possibility of a "loose alliance with conservative Protestants, Catholics and Orthodox Jews in seeking government aid to religious schools as well as opposing abortion, pornography and the acceptance of homosexual relationships or other sexual behavior outside marriage."[5]

Of course the news media conveyed some reservations about all this. But reservations are not equivalent to secularism. Consider our topoi: Applause for good works. Embrace of tolerance. Contempt for hypocrisy. Rejection of false prophets. Inclusion of worthy religious others. Appreciation of faith in things unseen. Concern about religious decline. These add up to a disposition that may be called establishmentarian, in the religious sense of the word. That is to say, when the news media turn to religion, their province is the entire community, not merely the interests of a particular faith or sect. Like all establishments, they tend to be interested in good order, and therefore are made uneasy by strong beliefs that threaten to disrupt society. Such prophetic functions as they perform are well within the bounds of convention: fostering charity, denouncing scoundrels, casting out madmen. The religion they prefer is domestic and generous and friendly, not revolutionary or hostile to the culture at large. It is no wonder that adherents of the latter sort of faith find their approach unsatisfactory.[6]

One such is Marvin Olasky, the University of Texas journalism professor who is perhaps the most acute evangelical Christian observer of religion and the news media. Like other evangelical critics, Olasky believes the media are possessed of an anti-Christian bias, but his is a root-and-branch critique that goes beyond the standard catalog of horribles. For him, the important question has to do not with how the news media deal with religion per se but with what kind of interpretive perspective they bring to the world at large. His journalistic hero is Nathaniel Willis, the early-nineteenth-century editor who treated all stories in terms of God's law and action in the world (chapter 1). In Olasky's view, the secularization of the news media began with the penny press, which in the 1830s drove religiously inspired publications like Willis's from the field as a source of news for the general public. This first foray into journalism for the masses substituted a humanistic perspective for a point of view that was theocentric—"centered on God's sovereignty, and not on chance, popular will, or the clergy."[7]

Olasky sees little hope for redemption in the mainstream media, for just as Cotton Mather (presumably) did not have to think twice about interpreting an earthquake as an act of "glorious God," so contemporary reporters cannot foreseeably be expected to conceive of news events in terms of religion's, or Christianity's, Great Story.[8]

> To the Christian, the atheist is leaving out basic fact due to his spiritual blindness. No easy compromise is possible when such fundamental presuppositions are battling each other. God shows Christians that He exists independently of our minds by acting on our minds from outside. Yet, if a person who had not had that experience is unwilling to accept the testimony of others, and thus assumes internally-generated psychological change rather than God's grace, he will see Christian fact as imagination, and Christian objectivity as subjectivity.
>
> In the long run, journalistic differences between Christians and non-Christians are inevitable.[9]

What Olasky proposes is a return to the Willis model of Christian journalism that unabashedly imposes a "biblical perspective" on the news. That does not mean piously avoiding sin and scandal. On the contrary, he would like to see a "Christian sensationalism without guilt" that "portrays man as sinner, fully responsible before God who requires obedience."[10] He thus applauds the media's exposure of Gary Hart's extramarital affair during the 1988 presidential campaign as providing "essential voting information" for those who want to make sure they are not casting ballots for an adulterer. He likewise, with reservations, applauds the coverage of Jim and Tammy Faye Bakker: "Christians capable of doing investigative reporting backed off, not wanting to help atheistic antagonists of the ministries. The result was that contributors did not receive information needed to make informed choices."[11] All in all, evangelical publications must be salty and hard-hitting; they should not "cast the net wider, minimize theological differences and cozy up to potential readers rather than to criticize them."[12]

It is well to recognize that there comes a point when no common journalistic discourse will be able to satisfy believers and nonbelievers alike or, perhaps more important, all groups of believers. Yet even editors as spiritually committed as Olasky may find virtue in reporting the news according to commonly accepted journalistic norms.

One general-circulation newspaper that has adopted an explicitly Christian point of view is the *Shippensburg* [Pa.] *News-Chronicle,* a semiweekly with a circulation of about six thousand. "I really think we're doing something completely unique in a general circulation newspaper," said Jim Curtis, who became editor in 1991, in a telephone interview in June 1994. "I view it as a tool of evangelism." Nonetheless, Curtis, who attends a Mennonite church, tries to confine his proselytizing to the editorial pages and a special weekly supplement called the "Good News Messenger." The supplement, which features uplifting stories, Christian book reviews, columns of spiritual advice, and announcements of services and revivals, is, according to Curtis, like an advertising circular; it can be thrown away by those who want no part of it. "I try in the news pages to keep it as neutral as possible, even lean the other way," he said. "I was taught that the job of editor of a newspaper was to be as objective as possible, tell both sides of the story, let the reader decide." Disengaging religious opinion from news in this way has quieted initial complaints from the community, he added, and circulation has held steady.[13]

This is not to suggest that standards of objectivity or newsworthiness are engraved in stone. Opinions shift, values migrate, and with them evolve the topoi that journalists pursue—for better or worse. In a roundtable discussion on the state of the media that appeared in the *New York Times Magazine* in mid-1994, ABC-TV's Jeff Greenfield cited the Gary Hart infidelity story as a kind of personal conversion experience.

> We were all saying the issue wasn't infidelity, the issue was judgment, and this guy from Texas [Olasky himself?] called me up and said, "Excuse me, but a man who stands in church in front of God and lies to the woman he's going to marry about how he will conduct his marriage, I don't want that guy in the White House." Now that may not be my standard, but there are millions of people for whom I suspect evidence of compulsive adultery is evidence of a character flaw so grievous that no matter how smart or courageous or committed he is, they don't want that guy in the White House. And I believe the press has a legitimate reason to inform the voter about that and let the voter make his choice.

Greenfield also noted that the women's movement had played its own part in justifying coverage of the sexual lives of politicians by arguing that the personal is the political — that it didn't matter how you voted on women's issues if you harassed women on the side.[14] One might add that, in a similar combination of forces, the Christian Right and the Feminist Left have both taken up cudgels against pornography. Such is the postmodern condition.

As the millennium came into view, journalists showed some awareness that, if the rough beast of religious revival was indeed slouching toward Bethlehem, they had better get up to speed. "Quietly, America's faith in religion is born again," ran the headline on a front-page *Boston Globe* story on April 4, 1994. "Seeking Solace and Spirituality, Many Turn to Meditation Books" was the *New York Times*'s front-page religion story on June 29. In 1994 as well, National Public Radio established a religion desk and ABC-TV became the first network to hire a full-time religion reporter. On the academic front, Northwestern University announced the establishment of a new center for Religion and the News Media.

Among those encouraging the journalistic community to embrace the world of faith was the television producer Norman Lear, well known too as the founder of the civil liberties lobby, People for the American Way. Addressing the National Press Club in December 1993

Lear pleaded not only for more coverage of religion, but also for coverage that would strengthen spiritual commitment: "I am hoping you will help to shine a light on the mounting religious fervor of our times, to help us understand not just the creeds and faith, rivalries that divide us, but that rich capacity for religious experience that unites us, to nurture the desire we all possess for some invisible means of support and to deliver to one another the way the universe delivers to us."[15]

Will the perception of revival lead to better informed or more sophisticated treatment of religion in the news media? Are there to be more harmonious relations with religious bodies and a decline in the media's secularist image? If nothing else, the news media do seem more inclined to deliver Lear's desired nurturance, or at least to put the common capacity for religious experience on display.

When *Life* explores prayer in America through a series of personal statements and polling data, it is reflecting a growing desire in the media to present the vox populi in as unmediated a way as possible. In a kind of journalistic populism, readers and listeners and viewers are presumed to prefer gazing into the mirror at themselves to having their attention directed elsewhere by a media elite. In daily practice, the doings of ordinary folks seem worthier of coverage than the ordinary business of institutions, be they governmental or ecclesiastical. City hall reporters no longer file two and three stories a day; it is no longer assumed that whatever happens at city hall should get into the paper. Religion news is no longer made simply by something happening in an important religious establishment. The Catholic bishop, the local presbytery, the rabbi of the largest synagogue in town no longer get covered just because they are who they are.

The tendency to scant the routines of institutional religion reflects not only prevailing journalistic attitudes but also academic ones. By the 1990s, it had become something of a sociological commonplace to regard American religious life as growing more fragmented, personalistic, and antinomian. In Robert Bellah et al.'s widely read *Habits of the Heart,* this spiritual style is epitomized by Sheila Larson, a young nurse who named her own self-regarding religion after herself. The authors claim that in late-twentieth-century America "Sheilaism" is "close to the norm."[16] Hoover, Hanley, and Radelfinger's study of religion reporting and readership likewise subscribes to this view, pointing to a new kind of American religion — "increasingly non-institutional" and finding expression "in diffuse and atomized locations and practices."[17]

Sheilaism may be overrated, however, at least as far as news appetites are concerned. In the national survey on which Hoover et al. study based many of its findings, the area of religion coverage that respondents said mattered most to them turned out to be the social and ethical positions and pronouncements of major faith groups. Religious controversies ranked well ahead of ecumenism and inter-religious cooperation, while surveys and polls on religious topics and individual faith experiences fell down near the bottom of the list. From this it is hard to avoid concluding that the American public is more interested in old-fashioned denominational politics than in the particulate spirituality of individuals.[18]

But we can't expect to go home again. As institutionally embedded as religious Americans still may be, our sprawling metropolises will never again be dominated by a few large downtown churches and synagogues. Although religious diversity is anything but new in American society, it has acquired a legitimacy that precludes a return to the days when definitive pronouncements on faith and morals could be derived from this or that pulpit or chair of theology. In all likelihood, coverage of religion will grow ever more thematic, issue-oriented, and trend-seeking. For this reason, it is especially important to understand the topoi that govern our awareness of the themes, issues, and trends.

The philosopher Charles Taylor has argued that philosophy cannot advance unless it works its way back to the historical roots of present-day assumptions.[19] In this book, I have looked at topoi historically as well as contemporaneously, with an eye to pointing out both their cultural rootedness and their contingent character. What should be clear is that coverage of religion based on a handful of topoi will necessarily fail to recognize other religious points of view. The more such points of view there are, the harder will they be to recognize. Under the circumstances, it is worth considering whether the best way to apprehend them is from a more critical vantage.

In 1935, the Presbytery of New Brunswick, New Jersey, tried J. Gresham Machen, Presbyterianism's leading conservative theologian, for disobedience. The official cause of action was that Machen, founder and president of the new, antimodernist Westminster Seminary, had joined with like-minded co-religionists to establish a new foreign missions board, thereby threatening to siphon funds from the denomination's existing Board of Missions. In the event, he was convicted and kicked out of the Presbyterian ministry. In a recent study of press coverage of the trial, James Barr, a writer at Pat Robertson's Christian Broadcasting Network, criticizes reporters for failing to come to grips with the underlying theological contest. To them, Machen was just the wayward fundamentalist son of a church trying to keep its bureaucratic affairs in order. But there were two journalists whom Barr praises for recognizing Machen as the knight errant of Christian orthodoxy he felt himself to be: the Unitarian editor of the *Boston Evening Transcript*, A. C. Dieffenbach, and the impious Mencken himself.[20] To a latter-day evangelical, the antitrinitarian and the atheist had seen what the unsecular, establishmentarian press could not.

If the news media were liberated from religious attitudes, would that make for better religion coverage? It is hard to imagine how such coverage would proceed, much less how it could be acceptable to the American public. Americans are a religious people, to judge by the amount of time we spend in religious institutions and the number of religious beliefs to which we subscribe. Religion news that did not in some sense defer to these institutions and beliefs would not merely enrage, it would confuse us.

At the same time, Americans do not expect the news media to promote one brand of religion over another. We live in a country whose founding charters proclaim religious liberty, whose longest-standing myth is the right of all to worship according to the dictates of their consciences, and whose reality since the beginning has been religiously pluralistic. Sectarianism, at least when it is recognized as such, cannot be permitted to reign in the public square.

In recent years, the impulse to remove the public square from sectarian control has, rightly or wrongly, come to be seen as an effort, largely successful, to exclude religion altogether from the common discourse. Many religious people regard themselves as waging war against a grim secularist tide. If this study has shown anything, however, it is that the public square, or at least the public bulletin board, has not been denuded of religion. To the contrary. Not only is American journalism reasonably attentive to matters of faith, but it also approaches these in what can only be described as a proreligious posture. Yet this is not to imply that the news media, much less the media generally, are religious as opposed to secular institutions. It is to suggest, rather, that employing mutually exclusive categories of "religious" and "secular" to characterize American culture today obscures more than it clarifies.

The topoi of religion news derive from religious sources and have their secular functions to perform. Like all topoi, they render the world morally comprehensible, and in America, morality is inextricably bound up with religion. At the same time, maintaining the moral order in America means not only embracing religion but also keeping it at arm's length. Journalists know that religion is dynamite; the topoi they use are moral packaging designed to keep the explosions to a minimum.

Just as the topoi intertwine the religious and the secular, so are they a joint creation of news recipients and news professionals. Like it or not, the prejudices and proclivities of the mass public will shape what they are and how they are deployed. Nor can journalism as we know it do without them. Especially in today's anti-institutional environment, in which coverage is tied less and less to what "merely" happens in a given place, topoi determine more than ever what constitutes news. For that reason, it is essential that those that lie to hand be as fair and reliable as possible.

If the topoi examined in the past few chapters serve some useful social ends, they undoubtedly capture a good measure of contemporary religious reality as well. As I have tried to show, however, these comfortable habits of thought all too often become mental straitjackets, preventing us from seeing what needs to be seen, showing us things that just aren't there.

Does focusing on pious good works give short shrift to what else religion can do in the world? Is tolerance the only touchstone for religion in the public square? Are we sure we know a hypocrite or a false prophet when we see one? Does a zeal for inclusion obscure the distinctive features of minority faiths? Do stories of supernatural belief lead away from ones about the ideological ends to which such belief is put? Does the question of spiritual decline (or revival) distract from real changes taking place in religious life?

The existing topoi need to be stretched. New ones need to be invented. Above all, stories need to be told simply because there is something interesting and different to tell. As John Darnton felt overwhelmed by the disparity between the daily experience of the people of New York and the tales told in the *New York Times,* so should we—

journalists and consumers of journalism—be better attuned to the disparity between religion as experienced by Americans and the tales the media have been telling about it. In a society, in a world, of insistent spiritual diversity, where more religious groups are playing public roles and new moral norms are vying with the old, we ignore this disparity at our peril.

NOTES

1. *Freethought Today,* September 1989.
2. Quoted in Alfred McClung Lee, *The Daily Newspaper in America* (New York: Macmillan, 1937), 195.
3. Edward Mortimer, "Islam and the Western Journalist," *Middle East Journal* 35 (Autumn 1981): 501–2.
4. *Time,* March 15, 1993, 25.
5. *New York Times,* May 7, 1993. The common cause against abortion and contraception made by the Vatican and some Muslim countries at the United Nations conference on population control in Cairo in September 1994 suggests that the idea of such an alliance was not farfetched.
6. For an account of the relationship between religious establishments and the establishmentarian tendencies of American secular institutions, see Leonard Silk and Mark Silk, *The American Establishment* (New York: Basic Books, 1980), 1–11 and passim.
7. Marvin Olasky, "Democracy and the Secularization of the American Press," in *American Evangelicals and the Mass Media,* ed. Quentin L. Schultze (Grand Rapids: Academie Zondervan, 1990), 60.
8. Olasky, "Democracy and the Secularization of the American Press," 62–63.
9. Marvin Olasky, *Prodigal Press: The Anti-Christian Bias of the American News Media* (Wheaton: Crossway Books, 1988), 71.
10. Olasky, *Prodigal Press,* 152.
11. Ibid., xii–xiii.
12. Olasky, "Democracy and the Secularization of the American Press," 64.
13. For an account of the remaking of the *News-Chronicle,* see Michael R. Smith, "Small-Town Upheaval," *Editor and Publisher,* May 30, 1992, 9–10.
14. *New York Times Magazine,* June 26, 1994, 62, 30.
15. Remarks of Norman Lear before the National Press Club, December 9, 1993 (Federal News Service, Inc.), 15. Four years earlier, Lear had urged public schools to nurture a sense of the sacred, saying, "While we civil libertarians have been triumphant in most of our legal and constitutional battles, I am

troubled that so many of us remain blocked or blind to the spiritual empti-
ness in our culture which the televangelists exploited so successfully." *New
York Times,* November 29, 1989.

16. Robert N. Bellah, Richard Madsen, William M. Sullivan, Ann Swidler,
and Steven M. Tipton, *Habits of the Heart: Individualism and Commitment in
American Life* (New York: Harper and Row, 1985), 221.

17. Stewart Hoover, Barbara M. Hanley, and Martin Radelfinger, *The RNS-
Lilly Study of Religion Reporting and Readership in the Daily Press* (Philadelphia: Temple University School of Communications and Theater, 1989),
8. In a follow-up study, Hoover, Venturelli, and Wagner reiterate this point
of view. See Stewart M. Hoover, Shalini Venturelli, and Douglas Wagner,
Religion in Public Discourse: The Role of the Media (Boulder: University of
Colorado Center for Mass Media Research, 1994), 13–16.

18. Hoover, Hanley, and Radelfinger, *The RNS-Lilly Study,* 71–75.

19. Charles Taylor, "Philosophy and Its History," in *Philosophy in History,* ed. Rochard Rorty, J. B. Schneewind, and Quentin Skinner (Cambridge:
Cambridge University Press, 1984), 17–30.

20. James Daniel Barr, "Newspaper Coverage of J. Gresham Machen's
Ecclesiastical Trial in 1935," unpublished thesis, Regent University, 1990, 64,
74–75.

Appendix

The following seven articles and columns, published between 1992 and 1994, are examples of how I have approached each of the topoi discussed in chapters 5–11. The brief introductions explain some of the considerations that went into writing the pieces, focusing in particular on how they conform to, and depart from, topical conventions. They are reprinted with permission from The Atlanta Journal *and* The Atlanta Constitution.

1. Good Works

Nothing represents good religion in the news media like good works, and the following story about the beginning of a citywide community organizing effort deals with religiously motivated good works on a grand scale. However, it challenges the conventions of the topos in two respects. Church folks are shown engaged in community action through an embrace of politics, rather than in the nonpolitical spirit of most religious efforts. In addition, the criticism by church leaders of Jimmy Carter's own effort in this area—religiously inspired and conventionally averse to politics—gives the story an unaccustomed edge.

INDUSTRIAL AREAS FOUNDATION

Churches Join Effort to Make Things Happen

GROUP LINKS BLACK, WHITE ATLANTANS

Zion's troops are mustering for an assault on the earthly city.

Last Sunday evening, 300 black and white Christians from a variety of denominations gathered at Druid Hills United Methodist Church to mix worship and political organizing.

There was preaching and praying and Bible reading. The air shook with the strains of "Marching to Zion" and "This Little Light of Mine." But the business at hand was to begin creating a secular organization that could change the face of politics in Atlanta.

Under the guidance of the Industrial Areas Foundation (IAF), a national non-profit agency that has helped birth 30 grass-roots organizations nationwide, Atlanta church folks are working to enable ordinary citizens to hold Atlanta's government and corporate leaders accountable for the welfare of the entire community. It's a painstaking process known, in the words of the Druid Hills service, as "Building the City of God: Moving Toward Justice."

It may eventually accomplish the sorts of things Jimmy Carter's Atlanta Project seeks to accomplish—better housing, education and jobs. But the approach is very different.

"It may just be the difference between old-fashioned top-down charity and a coalition that makes things happen," said Bishop Frank Allan of the Episcopal Diocese of Atlanta. "With the IAF, there's very little overhead, just a desk and a chair."

Bishop Allan said there's no reason church people should have to choose between the two efforts.

But for now, these churches are signing on with the IAF.

Twenty from Beulah Baptist Church, 15 from Holy Innocents Episcopal, 10 from Allen Temple AME, 50 from Peachtree Presbyterian. . . .

By that Sunday evening's end, 30 churches had promised to send more than 300 parishioners to two follow-up training sessions in February.

"I am excited and I thank the Lord for it," said Laura Hunter of Hunter Hills AME Church. "Because we have come together, and are coming together across racial lines."

SUCCESSES ACROSS THE U.S.

The IAF was started more than 50 years ago by Saul Alinsky, a flamboyant community organizer from Chicago. Since his death in 1972, it has found that churches, not unions or political wards, are the best building blocks for its kind of broad-based activism.

In San Antonio, an IAF affiliate has won more than $1 billion in government funds for rebuilding poor neighborhoods.

In New York City, IAF groups have built about 2,500 low-income houses.

In Baltimore, high school graduates with a 95 percent attendance record are guaranteed a job or college education.

"Not all [IAF organizations] have equal success," said Pablo Eisenberg of the Washington-based Center for Community Change, a non-profit agency that assists community-based organizations. "But on the whole they have shown that citizens can mobilize and influence not only their own lives but the institutions in their communities."

ATLANTA PROJECT OFFER REJECTED

John Hurst Adams made up his mind about Atlanta soon after arriving in 1988 as AME Bishop of Georgia.

"While our public relations image is extremely good, there are some appalling conditions," he said, citing deteriorated housing, unemployment and illiteracy. "I did not see any of these on the agenda of the city."

Bishop Adams, a member of the IAF board of directors, decided to put together a typical IAF sponsoring committee.

He rounded up the Catholic archbishop, the Episcopal and Lutheran bishops and leading African-American pastors such as the Rev. Tim McDonald of First Iconium Baptist Church, who was then executive director of Concerned Black Clergy.

"As opposed to a top-down thing, which so often happens, I really saw some permanency in this," said Harold Skillrud, the Lutheran bishop.

"Everything has led me to see real hope."

In October of 1991, the committee agreed to pay $30,000 to IAF so that organizer Arnie Graf could get started.

But before the month was out, former President Carter announced the Atlanta Project. At a meeting with Mr. Graf and members of the sponsoring committee, Mr. Carter invited them to join his effort. They declined, citing differences in approach.

The IAF, says Mr. Graf, wants to create a metrowide organization that agitates for its own agenda, relying solely on membership contributions.

"You can't be empowered on someone else's money," Mr. Graf is fond of saying.

The Atlanta Project aims to "empower" 20 designated neighborhoods, according to its director, Dan Sweat. Its multimillion-dollar budget comes from corporations and philanthropies.

"[The Atlanta Project] is going to raise an enormous amount of money, do a lot of things; but it will not correct the structural flaws in the city," said Bishop Adams. "I don't really see that group of people, who are the establishment in town, voluntarily giving up their power."

"Justice is love's demand." That is the IAF's motto.

In late 1991, Mr. Graf began spending a week every month in Atlanta, assessing interest in a full-scale organizing drive. A rumpled, blue-eyed man in his late 40s, Mr. Graf relied on the Rev. McDonald in overcoming the concern of black pastors that another "white savior" had descended on the community.

"I checked him out," the Rev. McDonald would tell the pastors. "He can't help it because he was born white."

In June, 90 clergy—half white, half black—had lunch at the Rev. McDonald's First Iconium Baptist Church and pledged to bring parishioners to a worship service at First Iconium.

"It hit me that this was professional," said the Rev. Gray Temple Jr. of St. Patrick's Episcopal Church in Dunwoody. "We were being asked to render account."

About 900 people from almost 50 congregations turned out for this initial gathering on Sept. 27 at the Rev. McDonald's church. In October, three follow-up training sessions at Druid Hills Methodist drew more than 250.

At the end of October, the sponsoring committee pledged another $30,000 for organizing and committed itself to raise a three-year budget of $465,000.

The training sessions in February will be followed by hundreds of one-on-one and small-group meetings, from which will emerge the beginnings of an agenda. Congregations will then decide whether to join the new organization.

Completing the process normally would take another year, but more time likely will be needed in Atlanta, Mr. Graf said.

"This city basically has been able to urban-renew and shrink and carve itself up with a limited amount of social protest," he said. "It makes organizing in Atlanta different. We need to go slower, so we understand it."

The go-slow approach leaves Woody Bartlett champing at the bit.

Director of community ministries for the Episcopal diocese, the Rev. Bartlett has been working on behalf of Atlanta's poor for 30 years. "Never have we gotten together as solidly across racial lines to do something together," he said. "I can taste it in my mouth, I can just taste it!"

January 30, 1993

2. Tolerance

This is one of a series of columns about a metro Atlanta county court-house. A week earlier, in a case that had generated a large amount of local publicity, the U.S. Supreme Court declined to review a lower court's decision requiring a plaque with religious texts to be removed from a courthouse two counties away. My aim was to show that religious sanctions are far more intimately embedded in the justice system than a plaque on a wall, but that these sanctions are problematic in an increasingly pluralistic community.

BIBLE IN COURTROOM POSING A PROBLEM

Judge Swears Off Traditional Oath;
but Agreement to Tell Truth Required

In its vain appeal to the U.S. Supreme Court, Cobb County argued that a plaque engraved with words of Jesus and the Ten Command-ments should be allowed to remain on its courthouse wall because "No society, nor any individual, can navigate the stormy seas of life for very long without a spiritual or moral compass and rudder. In this regard, religion serves a secular purpose."

No such plaque graces the DeKalb County Courthouse, but religion does serve a daily secular purpose in most courtrooms here and across the land, in the form of the Bible upon which witnesses are called to swear.

The custom derives from ancient common law, which required all witnesses to swear an oath to God. People who did not believe in a God who punished those who swear falsely were not allowed to give sworn testimony.

Then along came the Quakers, who refused to swear oaths on the grounds that this implied a double standard of morality—one for normal discourse, the other for courts of law and other formal settings. They also held that oaths violate the right to keep one's beliefs private.

Because of these religious compunctions, courts decided to permit witnesses to "affirm" as well as swear that they would tell the truth. "Swear or affirm" is now the formula used for, well, swearing in witnesses.

Putting one's hand on the Bible presumably makes witnesses fearful lest their words fail to measure up to the truthfulness of Holy Writ, and affords them the moral compass and rudder wherewith to navigate the stormy seas of cross-examination.

But DeKalb is a county with increasing numbers of people whose religious beliefs are unattached to either the Hebrew Bible or the New Testament. To at least one DeKalb judge, that made the use of the Bible for swearing-in problematic.

"I noticed that some people were uncomfortable with it, particularly Hindus and Muslims who didn't understand what the Bible meant," said Superior Court Judge Robert Castellani. "It made them feel uncomfortable."

To swear on a Bible put them in the position of believers in a faith they didn't profess. To refuse to so swear meant they risked the disbelief of jurors.

A devout Presbyterian who is married to a minister, Castellani also decided that he didn't like using the Bible "as a weapon" to encourage truthful testimony.

So, several years ago, he took it out of his courtroom. That, however, did not mean ceasing to require a formal agreement to tell the truth.

"The whole purpose," Castellani said, "is to give someone notice that serious sanctions will follow if you don't tell the truth."

The sanctions, to be sure, are the wholly secular ones that may result from committing perjury. But to all appearances, the ship of justice sails as straight in Castellani's Bibleless courtroom as it does in any other.

Of course, anyone who spends any time around a courthouse knows that, Bible or no Bible, half-truths and abject falsehoods are often uttered from the witness stand.

Castellani's court reporter, Lawson Thigpen, likes to say that rather than profane the Bible by lying, witnesses ought to swear on a dictionary. Especially witnesses in divorce cases.

June 9, 1994

3. False Prophecy

Written the day of the destruction of the Branch Davidians, the following news analysis piece was designed to put the tragedy in broader cultural context. I steered away from fixing blame with either a topos of false prophecy (David Koresh brought it on himself) or one of government misfeasance (federal law enforcement messed up). My goal, instead, was to show that American society has historically had difficulty handling challenges presented by unconventional religious behavior.

CULTS POSE A DILEMMA FOR SOCIETY

The fiery end of the Branch Davidian compound near Waco, Texas, raises troubling questions about the ability of law enforcement authorities—and American society in general—to deal with extreme expressions of religion.

The Branch Davidians had come to believe that former rock musician David Koresh was the Messiah, the salvation figure in Jewish and Christian tradition.

"In many segments of our society even the belief in a personal messiah is ridiculed," said Marc Stern, a lawyer with the American Jewish Congress. "On the other hand, Messianism is a real danger. That is really the dilemma. And we don't know how to deal with it."

The danger, he said, is exemplified in the Church of the Aryan Nation in Idaho, which stockpiled weapons and used them aggressively, yet evaded law enforcement for a long period by invoking the protection of the First Amendment.

Yet no evidence has surfaced thus far that Mr. Koresh and his followers planned to initiate armed violence with the weapons they had stored. He did teach that the end of the world was imminent, and that evil outside forces would have to be resisted by force.

Indeed, before the FBI moved in Monday, Mr. Koresh was said to be dictating the meaning of the Seven Seals from the Book of Revelation, the last book of the Christian Bible, which offers mystical but graphic accounts of the violent end of the world.

Under the circumstances, the final tragedy ought to have been anticipated, said Stephen Marini, a religion professor at Wellesley College.

"You roll up tanks and tell these folks you're only shooting tear gas and begin knocking down the buildings. Do you expect them to believe you? It looks a whole lot like religious persecution."

What originally caught the country's attention was not so much the group's supposed violation of gun control laws as its unconventional religious lifestyle. Former Branch Davidians alleged that Mr. Koresh had fathered numerous children by various women in the group, and that some children were being abused.

The women appear to have been willing participants, and social workers who visited the compound found no evidence of child abuse.

"If you believe differently, it's fine," said Catherine L. Albanese, a religious studies professor at the University of California at Santa Barbara. "Try to behave differently and you're in trouble."

In the 19th century, the U.S. government outlawed various religious practices, including Mormon polygamy and the Native American Sun Dance, in which dancers put skewers into their flesh. More recently, Christian Scientists have been prosecuted for refusing to permit their children to have medical care.

The challenge is to distinguish between religious acts that are merely alien or even repellent and those that actually violate laws or the rights of others.

To permit distress at a group's religious practices to influence law enforcement courts the kind of disaster that happened in Waco.

April 20, 1993

4. Hypocrisy

The scandal involving the huge, independent Pentecostal Cathedral of the Holy Spirit had received considerable media attention for some months when the following story was written. What began as an assignment to discover something about the scandal's effect on congregants turned into a report on, in effect, the church's theology of scandal. Without undermining the principal topos of hypocrisy, I wanted to let readers know that there was a theological justification for the cover-up—one that was central to the church's identity. Only after the story appeared did I discover that the doctrine of "covering" had a particular history within the Pentecostal movement (see chapter 1).

"COVER" DOCTRINE AT CORE OF APPEAL OF DEKALB CHURCH

TEACHING ENCOMPASSES SECRECY, AUTHORITY, PROTECTION — EVEN SPIRITUAL "INSURANCE"

A DeKalb County judge last week imposed a gag order on all parties to the slander and libel suit filed by the Cathedral of the Holy Spirit against several former members and staffers.

As a result, they are not to talk publicly about allegations of sexual misconduct that the church claims have driven away thousands of members.

But long before the gag order, the church taught the importance of keeping certain matters confidential. For example, in a handout distributed to church members the Sunday before the judge's action, church founders Earl and Don Paulk wrote that those who "dare drag" any sins involving the church "out from under the Blood of Jesus Christ do so at the peril of their own souls."

An extramarital affair with a church member acknowledged by the Rev. Don Paulk, as well as brother Bishop Earl Paulk's recent admission of such an affair from 1960, are among the news stories that have accompanied the church's turmoil this year.

After two decades of building a racially mixed ministry of social services, TV outreach, an academy and an immense $12-million, 7,700-seat cathedral in South DeKalb County, the church has lost half of its 12,000 members and almost half of its more than $1 million annual contributions, according to the lawsuit.

To understand the church, formerly called Chapel Hill Harvester, it is essential to grasp its distinctive doctrine of "covering." The concept involves not only concealment, but also spiritual authority and protection.

Current members and disillusioned former members alike, in talking about the church's current straits, describe covering as central to the church's theology and to its appeal.

"He shall cover thee with his feathers, and under his wings shalt thou trust," goes Psalm 91, and this image of spiritual authority de-

scends hierarchically at the cathedral from God through Bishop Earl
Paulk down to the family unit.

The congregation as a whole is divided into covenant communities
of a few hundred members, each "covered" by a pastor. The communities are in turn divided into groups of 25 "covered" by a deacon.
And at the family level, the husband is considered the spiritual covering of the wife.

Constant consultation with spiritual authority is the order of the
day at the church. Indeed, members are taught that if they do something wrong at the counsel of their spiritual authority, God holds the
counselor accountable, not them. On the other hand, those who act
independently are considered "rebellious spirits."

"No one can be your spiritual covering unless you give them that
position," said Melodie Ketchum, who met her present husband in the
church after arriving seven years ago with her two small children from
Texas "out of a real bad divorce situation." Covering, she said, "is like
an umbrella."

"It's mind control," said Pat Costello, who left the church a year
ago after 12 years. "It's a hard term, but I use it."

At the Cathedral of the Holy Spirit, covering has also come to
represent a kind of spiritual insurance policy. For some members, this
created an implied threat about the consequences of not answering
the church's continuing calls for money.

"You're almost fearful," said Cathy Brooks, who recently left the
church after nearly 20 years. "If you do not tithe, you're not covered.
Something bad will happen to you or your children."

To be covered is not only to be protected in spirit and body but
also to be pardoned, as in Psalm 32: "Blessed is he whose transgression
is forgiven, whose sin is covered." Over the years, Chapel Hill made
itself into a "city of refuge" — a place where substance abusers, unwed
mothers, homosexuals and fallen pastors from other churches could
be ministered to and have their sins covered.

Such covering extended to making a virtue of the concealment of
sin. "If I know someone that is having trouble in a certain area, if he

is trying to repent and change, and I tell people what is going on, that is wrong," said Rhonda Turner, a 10-year member who left the church in May.

Traditional Christian doctrine forbids publicizing the sins of the faithful lest the church itself be brought into disrepute. But in Christy Barrineau's view, this covering too easily became a self-serving "coverup."

So thoroughly does Chapel Hill cover its members that those who have left tend to describe their departure in terms of a failed marriage.

"I felt like I was divorcing," said Pat Costello. "I was depressed, I didn't know what to do with myself, I was angry. I know of people who actually had breakdowns."

And as with many divorced people, the idea of plunging into another union seems inconceivable. "I have no intention of ever joining another church, at least not for a long time," Ms. Costello said.

Christy Barrineau, who became involved as a 13-year-old in 1979 through the church's youth rock ministry, Alpha, has similar feelings. "I want to go some place where I can sing two hymns, hear a 15-minute sermon, shake hands and leave," she said. "The last thing I want to do is get involved."

To the Chapel Hill faithful, those who have slipped out from its protective covering seem dead in the spirit.

"I don't see the joy in those people's faces," said Joan Spivey, who joined the church 13 years ago. "If they were willing to listen to their spirit, I think they'd go back."

"It's called the pruning process," said Melodie Ketchum. "The people who have gone, they needed to go. We are going to come out stronger. Even if we lose the cathedral, we could start somewhere else with three or four hundred people. . . . I'm not worried a bit."

December 5, 1992

5. Inclusion

The following column shows the nonfundamentalist, nonfanatical side of Islam in an American context. It perfectly embodies the topos of inclusion; the story is that enlightened Muslims have selected the United States as the place to establish a center for promoting tolerance within their faith. The last part of the column, however, cuts against this Ameri-

*canism by calling attention to Muslim intellectuals who have, at some
risk to themselves, publicly opposed repression of free speech from within
Islamic countries.*

MAKING AN ATTEMPT TO STEER MARCH OF ISLAM

Excitement is not exactly endemic to academic conferences, but it
was palpable at the fourth annual Jewish-Christian-Muslim Scholars'
Dialogue held last weekend at Emory University. The dialogue, spon-
sored by the National Council of Christians and Jews, is dedicated
to bridging the theological distance between the world's three great
monotheistic faiths.

What caused the excitement was the unveiling of a plan by the Muslim scholars in attendance to establish a liberal Islamic center in Los
Angeles. Under the direction of an Egyptian theologian named Fathi
Osman, the Islamic Center for Research and Planning will consciously
oppose the form of Islam advocated by the late Ayatollah Khomeini.

Dr. Osman emphasized that a theocracy in which holy wars are declared, other religions oppressed and hands cut off for crimes is antithetical to Islam as he understands it. "It's important to know that not
all Muslims think that morality is the way it is practiced in Iran," he
said in an impassioned speech.

The idea is to bring Muslim communal leaders from around the
world to the center for one to two months, and inculcate a vision of
a modern, pluralist Islam. While the United States has only a small
number of Muslims (perhaps 2 million to 3 million), its traditions of
religious freedom and church-state separation make it the best place
for such an institution.

"Here there's not a problem of intimidation," Dr. Osman said.

At a time when fundamentalist Islam is on the march from Malay-
sia to Algeria, such a center would seem to be a lonely outpost indeed.
To be sure, for all its shortcomings, traditional Arab nationalism is
committed to the concept of a secular state. But the decline of this
ideology was dramatized during the Gulf War, when the secularist
Saddam Hussein wrapped himself in the garb of a Holy Warrior.

It's worth noting, however, that within the Islamic world itself Muslim voices continue to be raised in support of religious pluralism and
liberal democracy.

Last year, Sadik al-Azm, a Syrian philosopher, published a lengthy
article celebrating Salman Rushdie as a Muslim Rabelais, Voltaire and

James Joyce wrapped into one; like them, Mr. Rushdie creates sophis-ticated literary critiques of his religious tradition. Mr. al-Azm, who got into trouble with the Lebanese authorities a quarter-century ago for writing a critique of Islam, argues that Mr. Rushdie didn't spring from nowhere.

Intellectual life and cultural activity in the Muslim world is not as "Islamically conformist, religiously unquestioning and spiritually stagnant" as Westerners imagine, Mr. al-Azm says. Indeed, pro-Rushdie petitions have been signed by many Muslim intellectuals, not only in the West but in Syria and Lebanon.

Mr. al-Azm contests the common Western view that "religious tol-erance, democracy, free speech and all that goes with them" are alien and repellent to Muslim societies and cultures. "Although religious tolerance was conquered for the modern world in Europe," he writes, "it is a common good and not just a 'deep Western value' inaccessible to non-Westerners and to Muslims in particular."

There may be some wishful thinking here, but the history of Islamic civilization contains more than enough precedent on which to build tolerant democratic regimes.

January 9, 1992

6. Supernatural Belief

The following article, which ran as a sidebar to a longer story on Catholic apocalypticism, explores the place of Marian devotion and apparitions within the Catholic church. This was an aspect of the Conyers story (chapter 10) to which the newspaper had devoted no attention in the course of nearly three years of coverage. I was at pains to avoid imply-ing that Marian spirituality was just church politics, and thus returned at the end to the familiar topos of supernatural belief. The religion editor felt that the story should give the skeptical no cause to think us credu-lous, and believers no cause to think us skeptical.

CATHOLIC DEVOTION TO VIRGIN
TAKES MANY HISTORICAL TURNS

Once upon a time, the Virgin Mary was celebrated for her indul-gence to wayward souls. In the great miracle collections of the Middle

Ages, she takes pity again and again on sinners whose only merit is their special devotion to her.

But at Conyers and other contemporary apparition sites around the world, Mary's messages have been stricter, gloomier — and critical of recent trends in the Catholic Church.

According to Nancy Fowler and others who say they hear from her, Mary denounces the sinfulness of the world and warns that the church has strayed from the straight and narrow of traditional doctrine.

I think she's responding to the times," said Ted Flynn, whose book, "The Thunder of Justice," outlines an apocalyptic scenario in which Mary plays the role of prophet of doom. "The Catholic Church is going through the passion of Jesus Christ. The church is dying in its present form."

Since Protestant reformers did away with the cult of Mary, Catholic devotion to the Virgin has been enmeshed in church politics.

In the 19th century, popes promoted Marian doctrines as part of a campaign to resist the secularization of Western culture. In the 1950s, Marian piety was enlisted in the church's war against communism.

DOWNPLAYED AFTER VATICAN II

But Mary tended to be downplayed after the Second Vatican Council of the early 1960s, which sought to adapt the church to the modern world and promoted ecumenical contacts with Protestants and non-Christians.

"Since Vatican II, there has been a fairly systematic elimination of certain symbols, of certain gestures, rituals, traditions that really were and are deeply ingrained in ordinary Catholics," said Allan Deck, a Jesuit theologian at Loyola Marymount University in Los Angeles.

"We are paying a heavy, heavy price for having perhaps moved too cavalierly, too precipitously in that direction."

But to Richard McBrien, a theologian at the University of Notre Dame, the current revival of Marian spirituality is an unwelcome throwback.

"These are Catholics who are basically stuck in a time warp," McBrien said. "It's really part of an effort to challenge Vatican II Catholicism and roll back as much of it as possible."

The current Marian movement traces its lineage back as far as the famous apparition of Guadalupe in 1531, when the Virgin appeared to a converted Mexican Indian. But its most important ideological antecedent is Fatima, Portugal, where in 1917 she appeared to several children.

At Fatima, Mary allegedly made remarks about the conversion of Russia that over the years have assumed apocalyptic significance. She is also supposed to have disclosed a "third secret" that the Vatican has never revealed.

WAY "OF APPROACHING THE DIVINE"

Marian apparitionists, who operate centers in several American cities, represent one of several streams of conservative Catholicism, according to William Dinges, a religion professor at the Catholic University in Washington.

Other traditionalists, such as those who favor a return to the Latin Mass, are suspicious of apparitions, which represent an influx of supernatural power unmediated by the church hierarchy.

"They don't seem to be too enamored of these Marian goings-on," Dinges said. "The Marian stuff is charismatic authority, as opposed to correct doctrine."

It is unclear how much the church politics or the prophecies of doom matter to the thousands of rank-and-file Catholics who bring their faith, their illnesses and their Polaroid cameras to apparition sites.

A large proportion of the Conyers pilgrims are Hispanics from south Florida, for whom devotion to Mary has always been a central part of Catholic spirituality.

"They expect healing through miraculous events; they expect the reality of a transcendent God who makes himself known in unusual ways," said Deck, the Jesuit theologian.

"The Virgin Mary has always been their way of approaching the divine. It's par for the course."

June 12, 1994

7. Declension

Reporting on megachurches often focuses on their marketing of religion to baby boomers concerned with creature comforts — generally considered a bad sign of the times. My interest was to minimize that element of the story, and instead to focus on one megachurch's impact on its sur-

rounding community. I did consider the standard question about size, but without disputing that a megachurch may be impersonal, I tried to show how the intense experience of community that small churches afford is not necessarily all sweetness and light.

THE CHURCH THAT SWALLOWED DACULA

How Hebron Baptist Caught the Wave of Suburban Growth

POWERFUL INFLUENCE: WITH ROUGHLY HALF
OF THE CITY'S 2,700 RESIDENTS ATTENDING HEBRON,
THE ONCE SMALL CHURCH IS A FORCE TO BE RECKONED WITH

As Dean Butler likes to tell it, when he joined Hebron Baptist Church in 1961 with his wife and five children, they boosted weekly attendance by 10 percent.

Today, the little white frame church off Dacula Road is gone, replaced by a 1,300-seat auditorium. A Church Life building is under construction and there are plans to replace the auditorium, which was built three years ago.

In 15 years, the smallest of the dozen small Baptist churches in and around Dacula has grown to nearly 3,000 regular worshipers.

Mr. Butler, 67, who used to put GM cars together in Doraville, admits he misses the small church "in a way." But, he says, "ain't no way I'd go back to it."

Hebron's is a classic story of church growth on the metro Atlanta frontier. In the 1980s, when Gwinnett was the fastest growing county in America, Hebron caught the wave perfectly.

But in doing so, it powerfully affected the spiritual infrastructure of its community. These days, roughly half of Dacula's 2,700 residents attend Hebron.

GROWTH BECAME TOP PRIORITY

Ten years ago, Nelson DeBrosse's 14-year-old daughter was killed in an auto accident. The first person to show up at the hospital was Hebron's pastor, the Rev. Larry Wynn, who had begun going out on rounds with the Dacula Fire Department.

"I believe God put him there for a reason," said Mr. DeBrosse, who was raised Roman Catholic but had not attended church since moving to Gwinnett from Ohio five years before. "It was that love that we found in him that led us to Christ."

And it led them to become members of Hebron.

Growth became Hebron's top priority within months of the arrival of the Rev. Wynn, then a 24-year-old graduate of Mercer University in Atlanta, in 1977.

"The feeling from the beginning was that the purpose of this church was to reach out to as many people as we could," said the Rev. Wynn, who last fall was elected president of the Georgia Baptist Convention. "Yes, it was very comfortable to grow up in a church where you knew everyone. But then you read the Bible, and it wasn't what the Bible said."

Along with aggressive evangelism, the church gradually expanded its style of worship from traditional hymn-singing to include the rock-influenced music of contemporary Christian gospel. It also initiated counseling ministries, support groups and "life skills" seminars.

"Our parents didn't have the influence of TV," said Judy Gordon, a 20-year member of Hebron who serves as the church's financial officer.

Baby boomers won't be satisfied, she said, "unless your church really offers something that will compete with what the world offers them."

YOUTH OUTREACH IS STRONG

CRITICAL TO HEBRON'S SUCCESS
HAS BEEN ITS OUTREACH TO YOUTH

"We want to be part of the community," said the Rev. Wynn, whose wife teaches at Dacula Middle School. "If you're only a community within yourself, I don't think you're able to fully carry out the commission of Christ to go out into the world."

Lisa Knutson, whose family attends Dacula's small United Methodist Church, has run into Hebron's performance of that commission.

Last year, her older daughter brought home from the middle school a pamphlet Hebron friends had given her that claimed a person could not be saved unless baptized by complete immersion.[1] It took a long family discussion to convince her that that was not necessarily the case, Ms. Knutson said.

"We would not want anyone in our church to be offensive," said the Rev. Wynn, whose own manner is boyish and friendly. "But I'd rather kids be fired up about their church than a lot of things they could be talking about."

Derek Spain, 21, a valedictorian and football star when he was at Dacula High, was recently hired to run Hebron's 200-member high-school youth ministry. He likes to hang out at school and have lunch with the students.

"I live their lives with them," he said. "I don't go down there to 'P.R.' our church, [but] to be a regular person."

Hebron's influence is clear to Steve Parr, who directs the church's youth ministries.

"There's not a school in the county with a stronger moral base than Dacula High School," he said. "We've had a part in it."

Not all the local clergy are so enthusiastic, however.

"You're talking about community control," said the Rev. R. Page Fulgham of First Baptist Church in nearby Lawrenceville. "This thing is almost like two-thirds of the football team go to Hebron. And yes, they do pray in the schools. They sort of saturated the whole culture. Which is a way to win."

"A FEEDER CHURCH FOR HEBRON"

Hebron's evangelism has likewise affected neighboring churches, First Baptist Lawrenceville among them.

The Rev. Fulgham, who professes admiration for the Rev. Wynn, reckons that a couple of dozen families have left his church for Hebron.

"I joke about it that our church is a feeder church for Hebron," he said. But, he admits, "they're reaching people we wouldn't reach."

Five years ago, Mark Chandler, pastor of First Baptist Dacula, set up a youth program. Within three years, all the participants had drifted away to Hebron.

But the Rev. Chandler takes comfort in the fact that his 125-member independent Baptist church offers an intimacy that Hebron can't match.

"If they need me in the middle of the night, I'm there," he said.

Ironically, in the small churches, intimacy can breed divisions — over theology, style of worship or generational control. Steve Ferguson, pastor at nearby Ebenezer Baptist, recognizes, with some frustration, that Hebron offers a haven from these kinds of divisions.

"Some of those people were very involved in their church activities," he said. "Then something happens and they get offended and hurt, and it's easier to go to Hebron where you don't get involved, where you can stay on the fringe."

At Hebron, they try to minimize the anonymity that goes with size. Every Wednesday night, its members meet in 120 Bible study groups, which foster not only learning but "bonding" as well. Members say that Hebron retains a "small church feeling."

NO INTENTION OF SLOWING DOWN

But for many suburbanites of the baby-boom generation, that feeling may not be so important.

"A lot of people don't want to be hugged," said Lyle E. Schuller, author of *The Seven-Day-a-Week Church,* a 1992 book on modern American megachurches.

"I think we are living in a world that has taught people to be comfortable in a world of big institutions."

Hebron, whose annual budget is now $1.9 million, aims to have 3,400 regular worshipers by the end of 1994, and has no intention of stopping there.

Indeed, the new subdivisions popping up around Dacula pose a continuing challenge. Because of school rezoning two years ago, the proportion of Hebron children in the Dacula schools has dropped from one-half to one-third, church officials estimate.

And the newcomers have begun to resist Hebron's religious hegemony.

Every May, the Dacula recreation board would suspend its Spring softball season during Hebron's annual Starlight Crusade revival.

Last year, however, some new board members objected to the practice and a compromise had to be worked out. Softball would continue through crusade week, but any team that could not field enough players would be permitted to reschedule rather than forfeit a game.

"I was glad to see that," said Lisa Knutson. "Softball was not closed down for any other church."

February 13, 1993

NOTE

1. After the article appeared, there was some concern in Georgia Baptist circles about whether Wynn, as president of the convention, was teaching the necessity of total immersion baptism for salvation. In a letter to the editor (February 20, 1993), Wynn said that Hebron neither held to that belief nor had produced a pamphlet to that effect.

Index

___

MARK SILK received his higher education at Harvard University, earning a Ph.D. in history in 1982. He taught as a lecturer on history and literature at Harvard from 1982 to 1985, then spent two years as editor of the *Boston Review*. He joined the staff of the *Atlanta Journal-Constitution* in 1987. He is the author of *Spiritual Politics: Religion and America since World War II* (1988) and (with Leonard Silk) *The American Establishment* (1980).